HAL•LEONARD

GUITAR
PLAY•ALONG

VOL. 77

Bluegrass

ISBN 978-1-4234-2119-1

HAL•LEONARD®
CORPORATION
7777 W. BLUEMOUND RD. P.O. BOX 13819 MILWAUKEE, WI 53213

Visit Hal Leonard Online at
www.halleonard.com

CONTENTS

Duelin' Banjos

By Arthur Smith

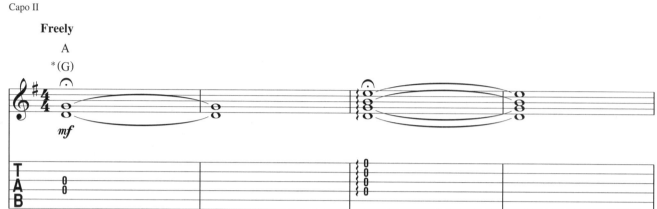

*Symbols in parentheses represent chord names respective to capoed guitar.
Symbols above represent actual sounding chords. Capoed fret is "0" in tab.

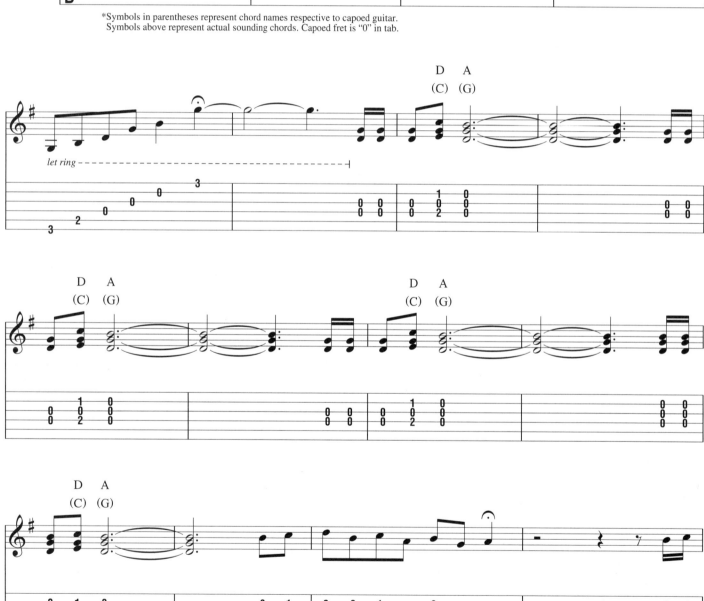

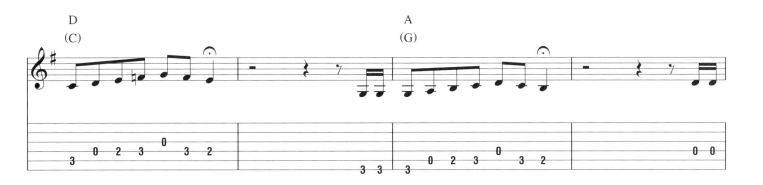

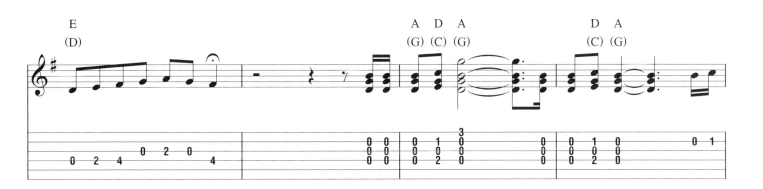

Moderately ♩ = 112

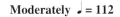

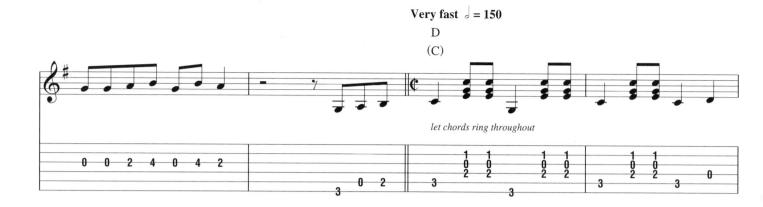

let chords ring throughout

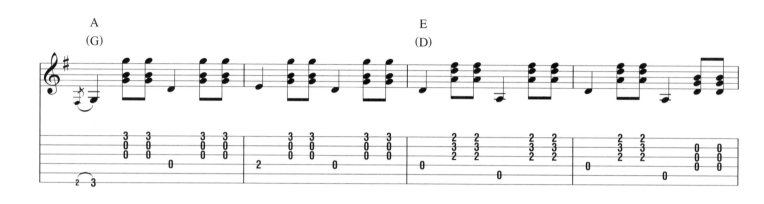

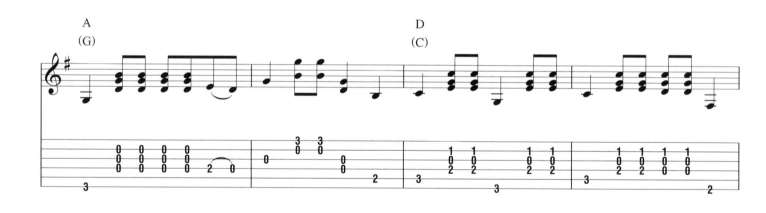

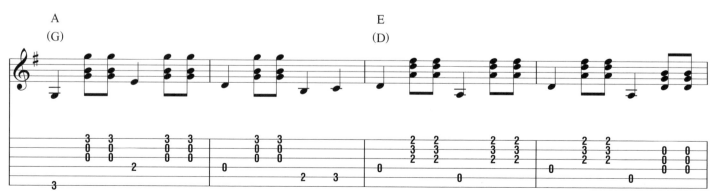

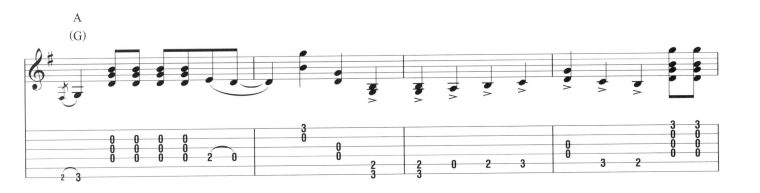

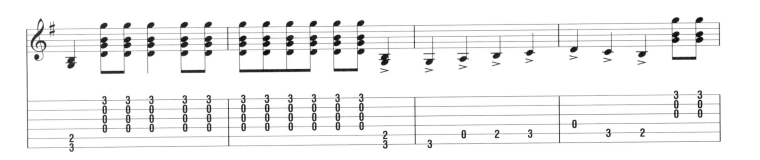

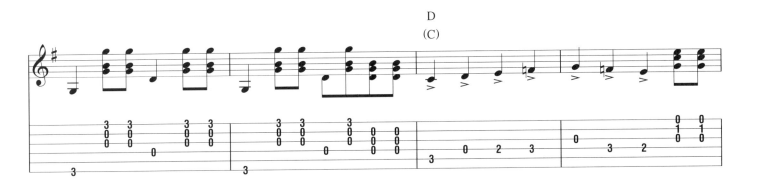

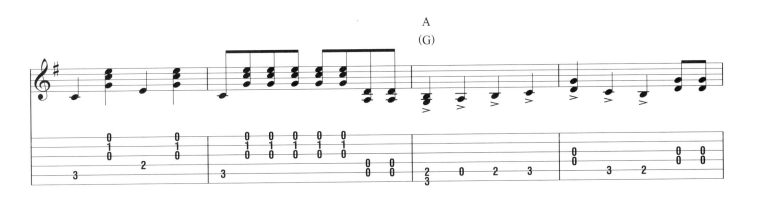

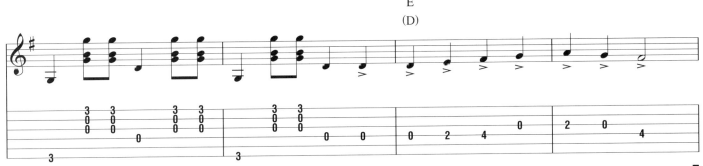

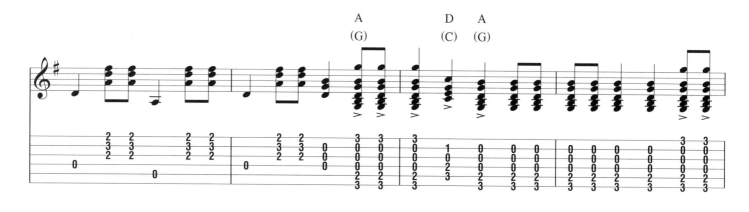

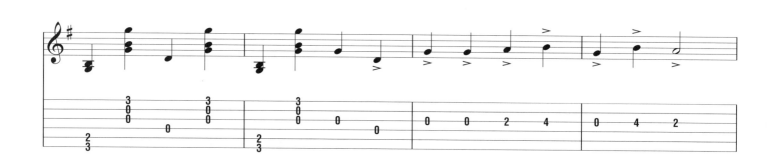

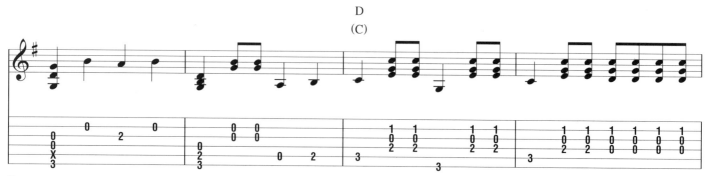

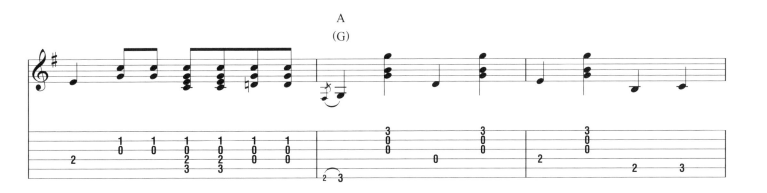

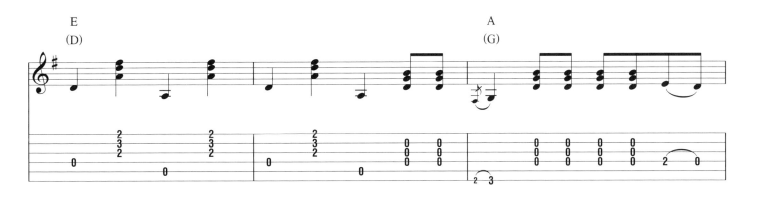

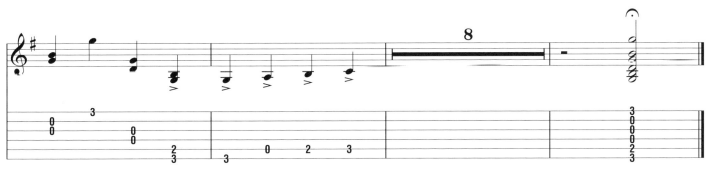

Foggy Mountain Breakdown

By Earl Scruggs

Open E tuning:
(low to high) E-B-E-G♯-B-E

Capo III

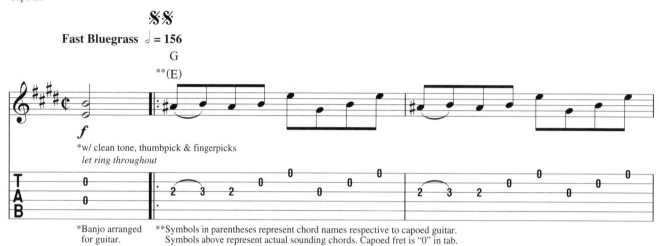

w/ clean tone, thumbpick & fingerpicks

let ring throughout

*Banjo arranged for guitar.

**Symbols in parentheses represent chord names respective to capoed guitar. Symbols above represent actual sounding chords. Capoed fret is "0" in tab.

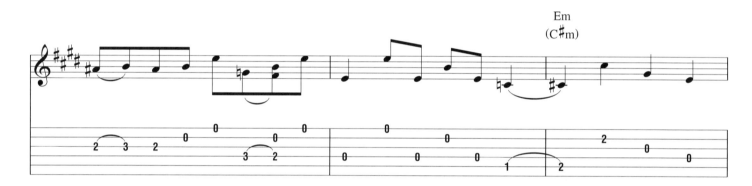

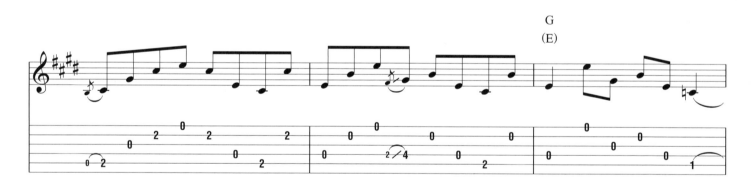

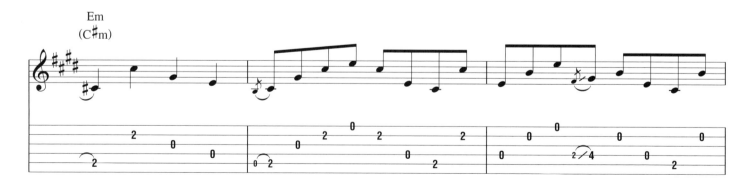

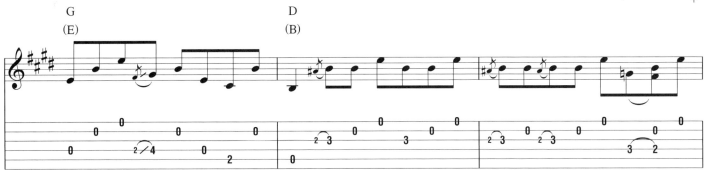

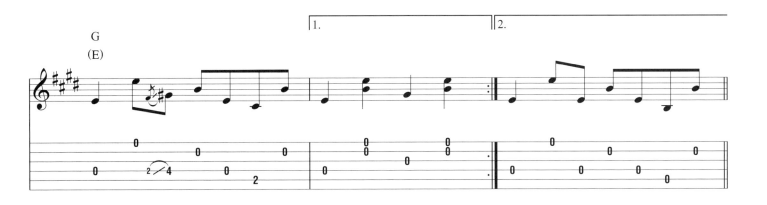

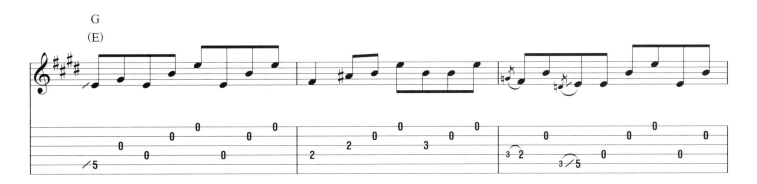

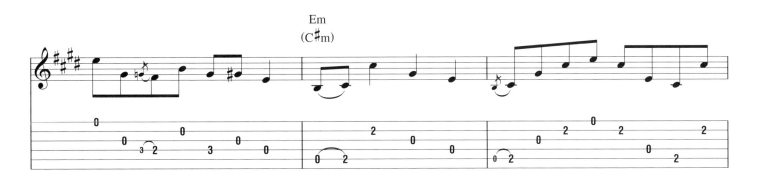

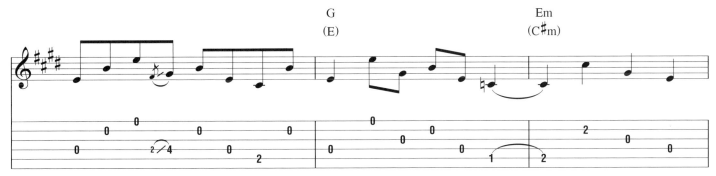

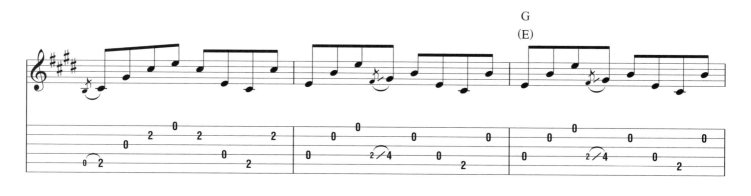

2nd, 3rd, & 4th times, substitute Fill 1

Fill 1

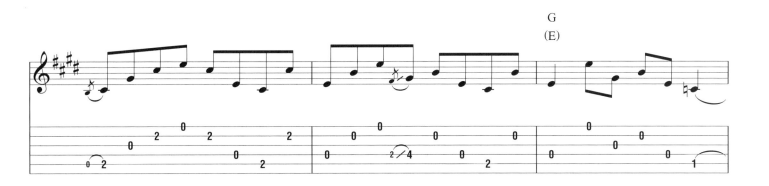

Em
(C#m)

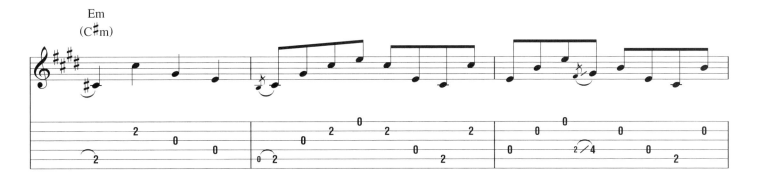

G   D
(E)   (B)

1.   2.

2nd time, To Coda 1 ⊕

G
(E)

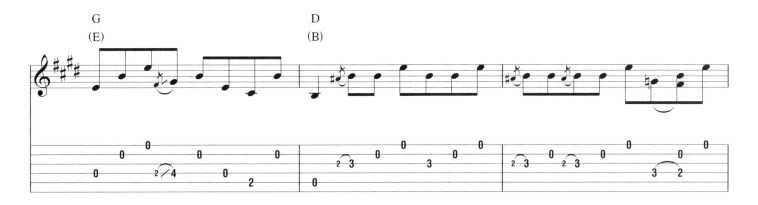

G
(E)

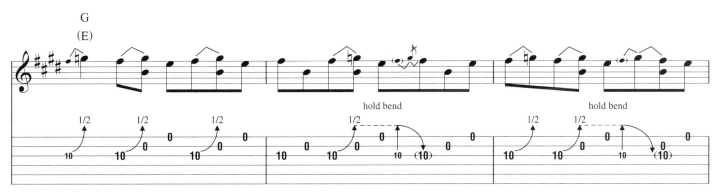

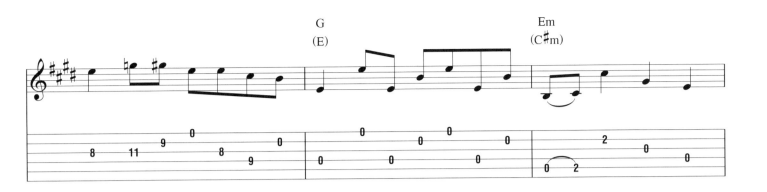

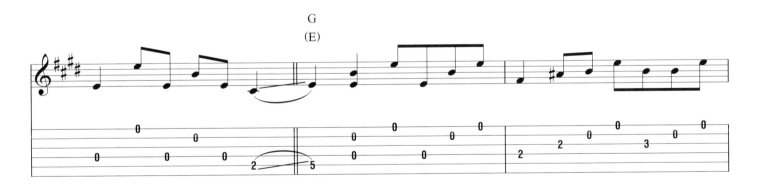
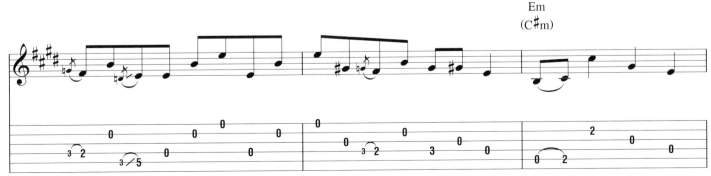

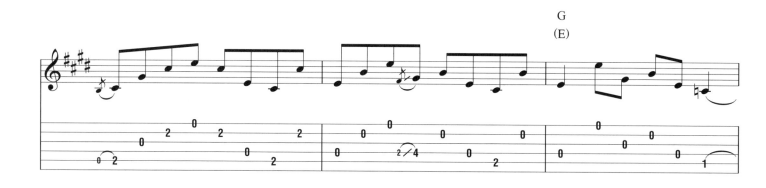

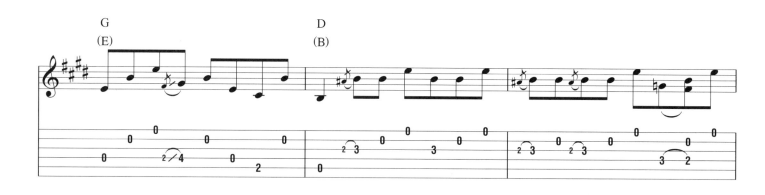

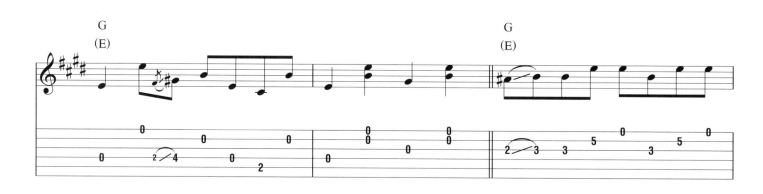

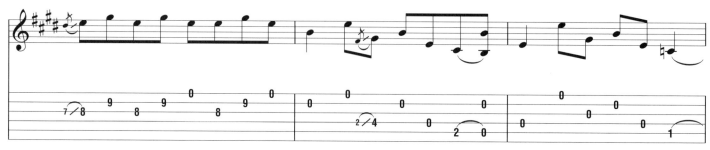

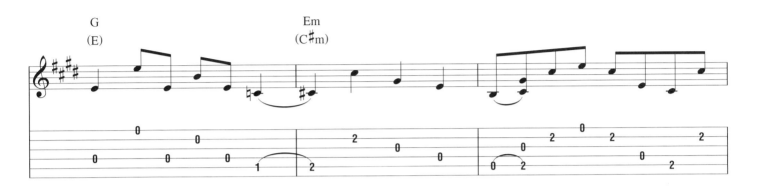

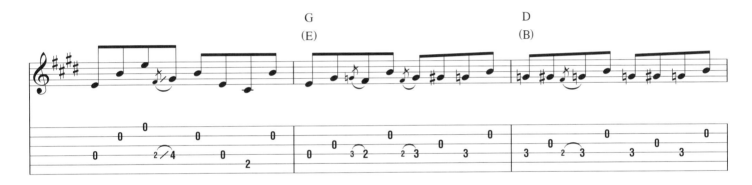

D.S. al Coda 1
(take repeat)

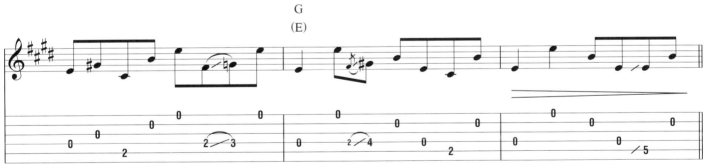

 Coda 1

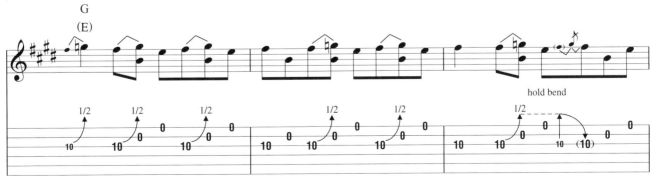

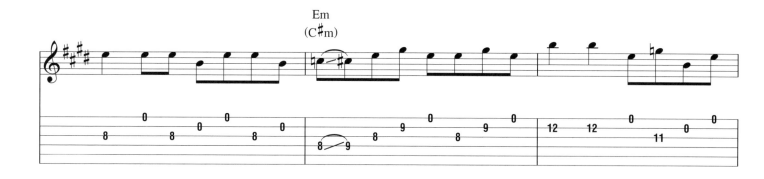

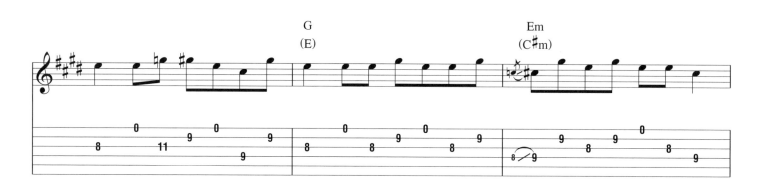

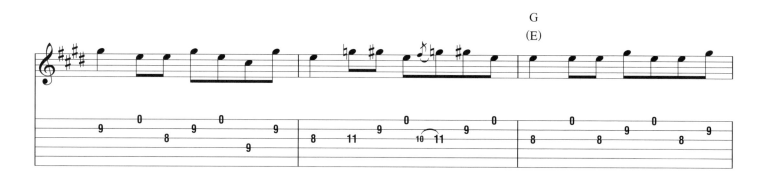

D.S.S. al Coda 2   **Coda 2**

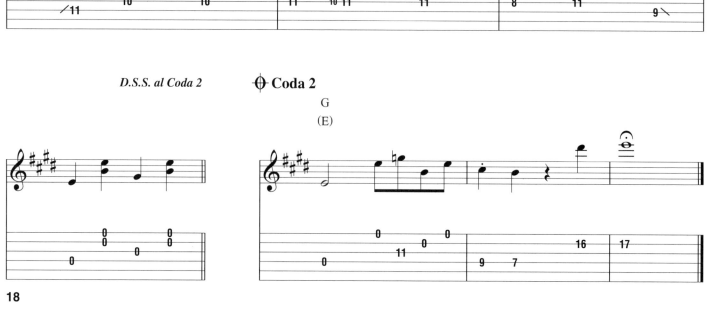

18

I Am a Man of Constant Sorrow

featured in O BROTHER, WHERE ART THOU?

Words and Music by Carter Stanley

Capo I

Intro
Moderately ♩ = 86

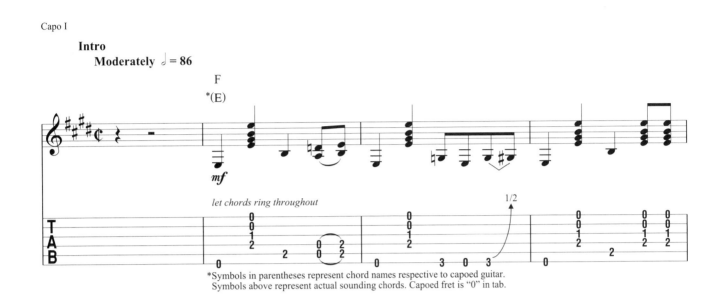

*Symbols in parentheses represent chord names respective to capoed guitar.
Symbols above represent actual sounding chords. Capoed fret is "0" in tab.

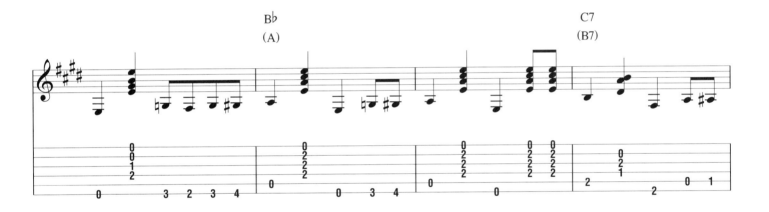

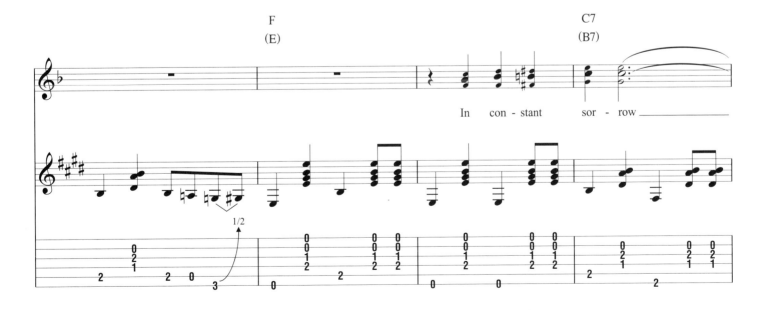

In con-stant sor-row ___

all — through his — days.

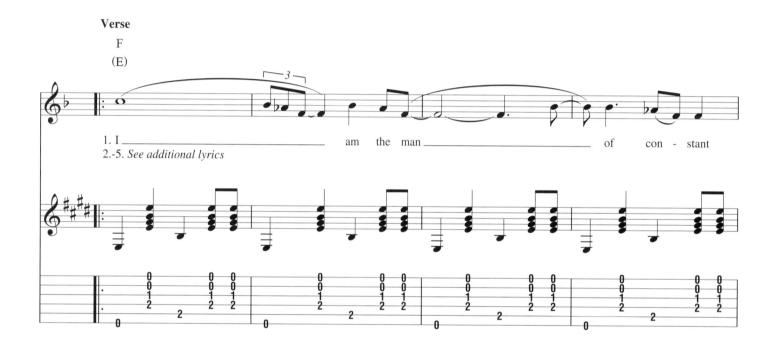

Verse

1. I _____ am the man _____ of con - stant
2.-5. *See additional lyrics*

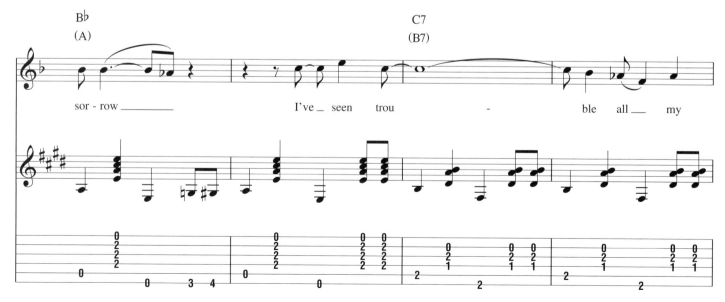

sor - row _____ I've _ seen trou - ble all _ my

20

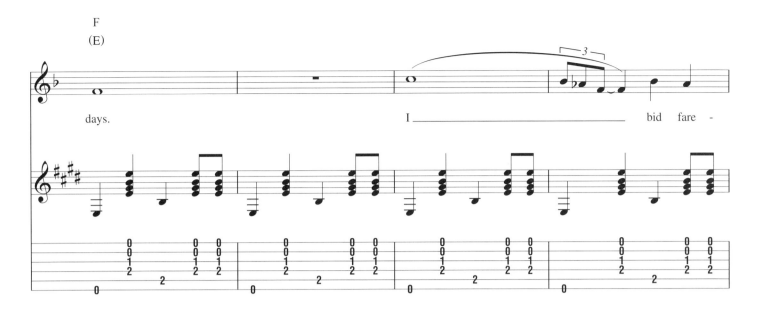

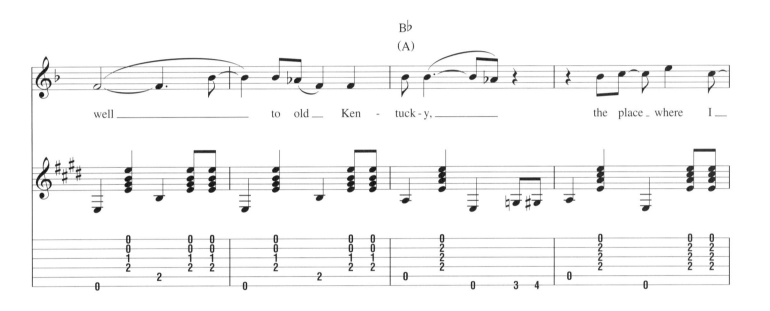

Interlude

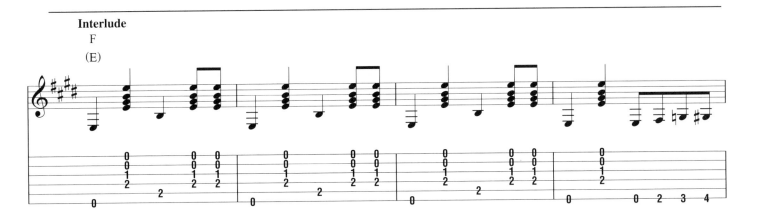

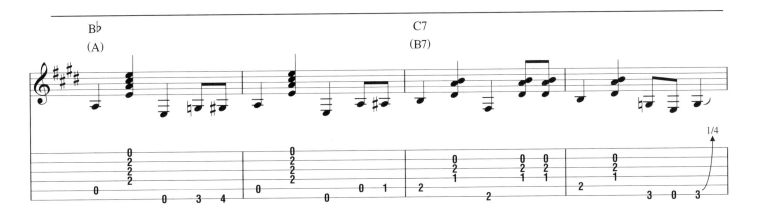

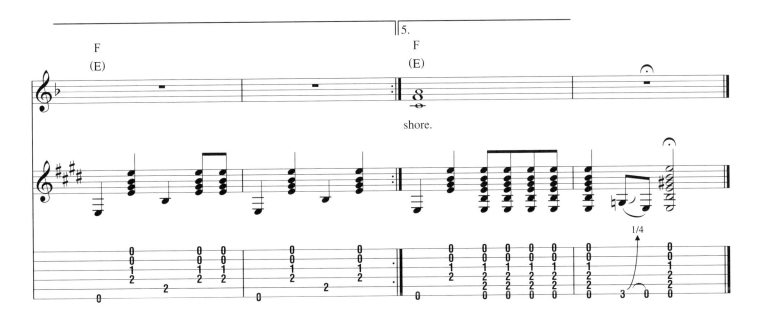

shore.

Additional Lyrics

2. For six long years I've been in trouble.
   No pleasure here on earth I've found.
   For in this world, I'm bound to ramble.
   I have no friends to help me now.
   He has no friends to help him now.

3. It's fare thee well, my old true lover.
   I never expect to see you again.
   For I'm bound to ride that Northern Railroad.
   Perhaps I'll die upon that train.
   Perhaps he'll die upon this train.

4. You can bury me in some deep valley,
   For many years where I may lay.
   And you may learn to love another
   While I am sleeping in my grave.
   While he is sleeping in his grave.

5. Maybe your friends think I'm just a stranger.
   My face you never will see no more.
   But there is one promise that is given,
   I'll meet you on God's golden shore.
   He'll meet you on God's golden shore.

Gold Rush

Words and Music by Bill Monroe

Capo II

Intro
Fast Bluegrass ♩ = 138
*N.C.

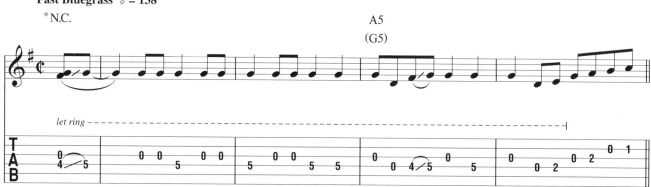

*Symbols in parentheses represent chord names respective to capoed guitar.
Symbols above represent actual sounding chords. Capoed fret is "0" in tab.

Theme
A
(G)

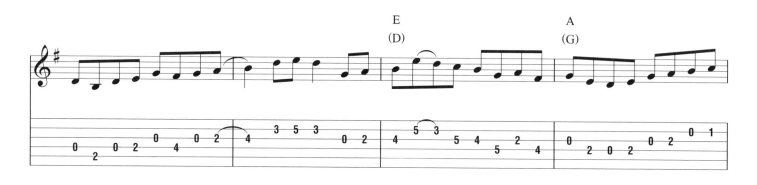

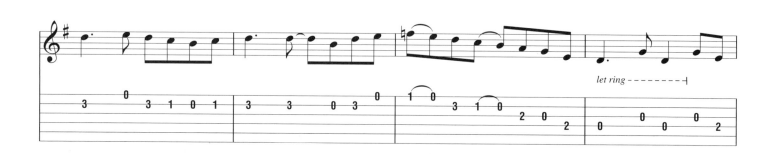

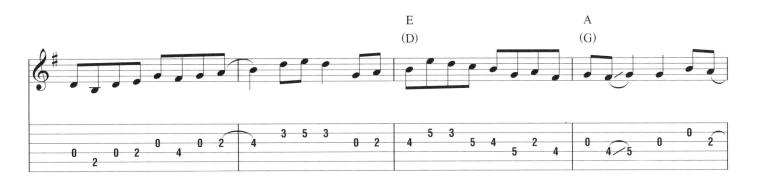

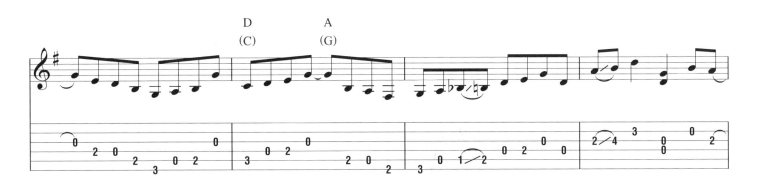

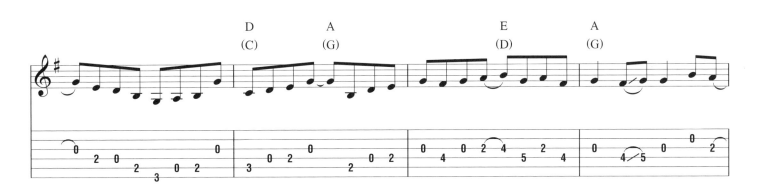

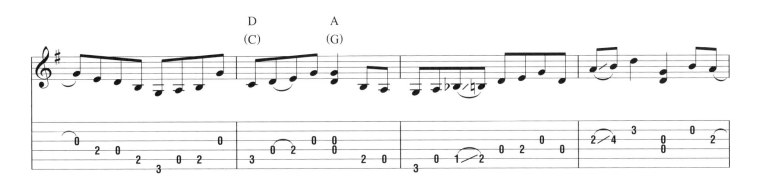

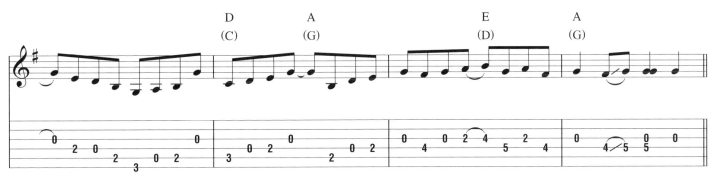

Fiddle Solo

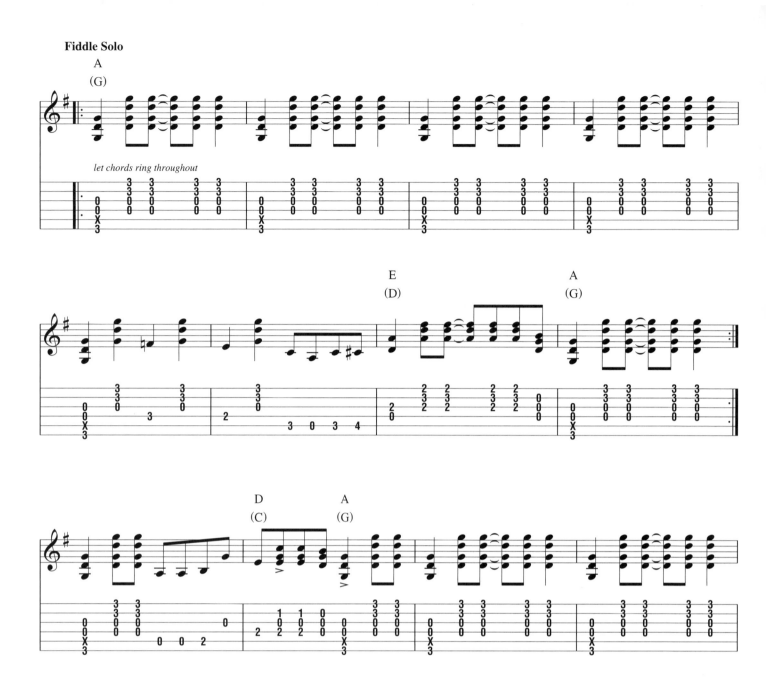

let chords ring throughout

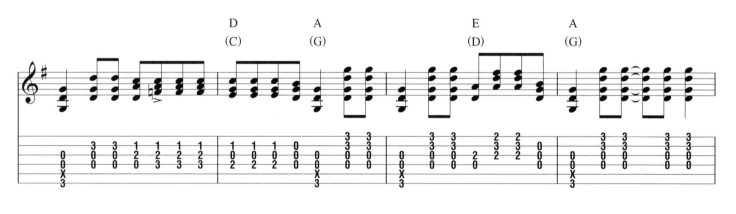

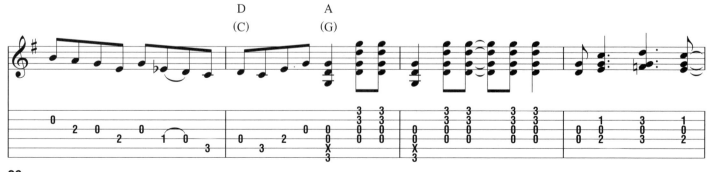

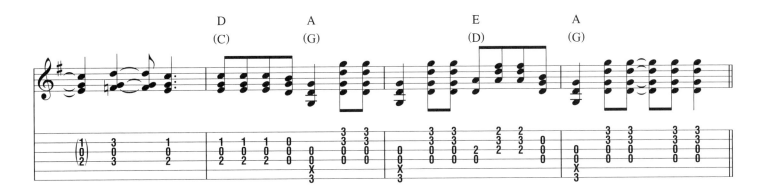

Mandolin Solo

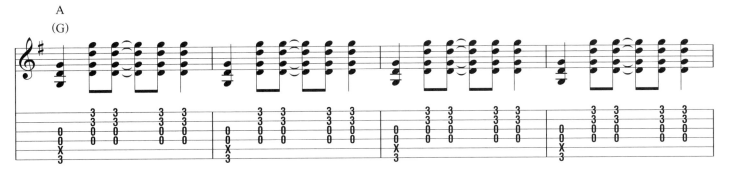

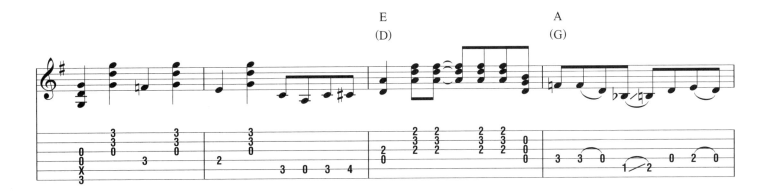

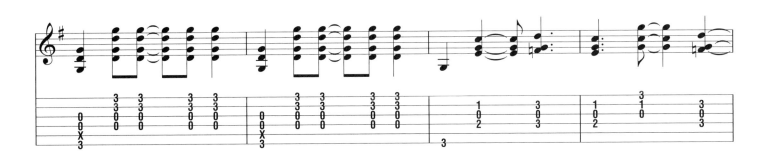

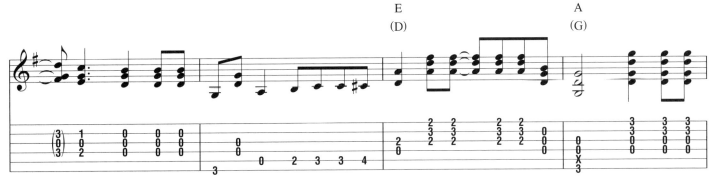

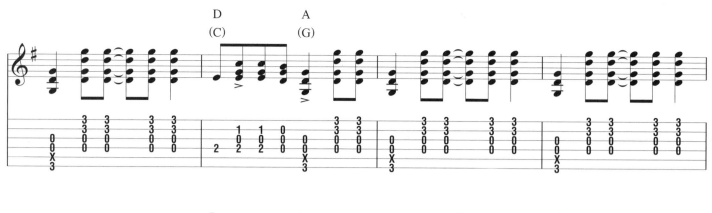

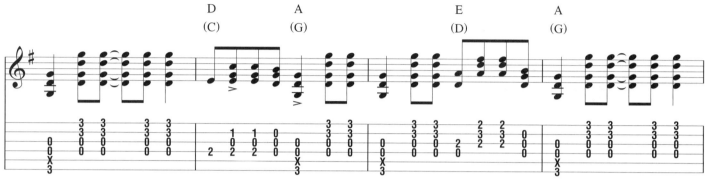

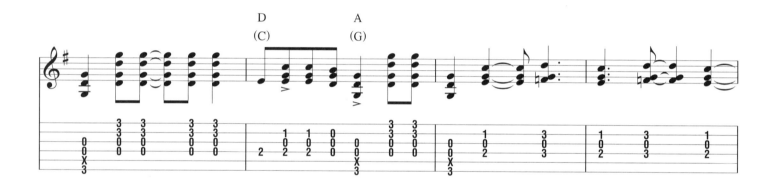

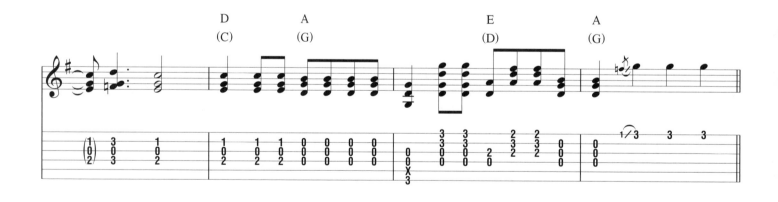

Guitar Solo

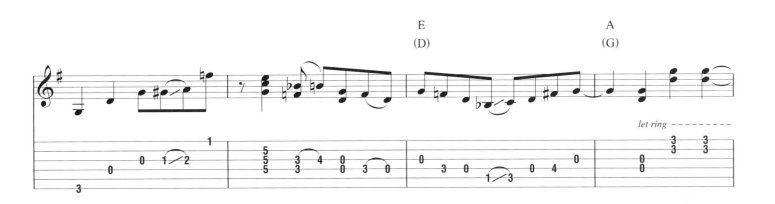

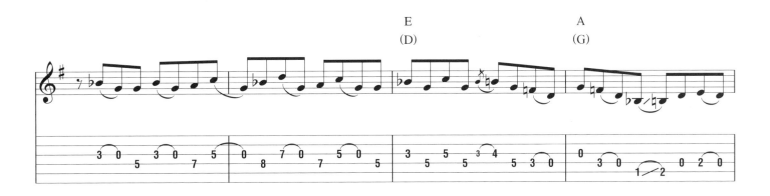

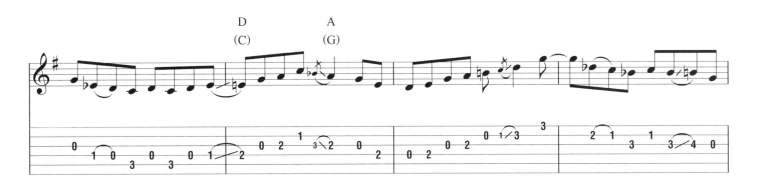

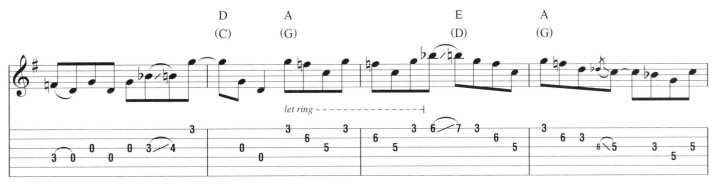

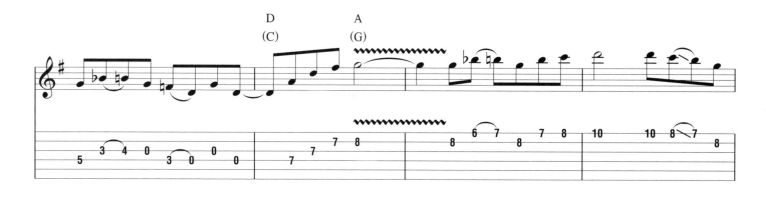

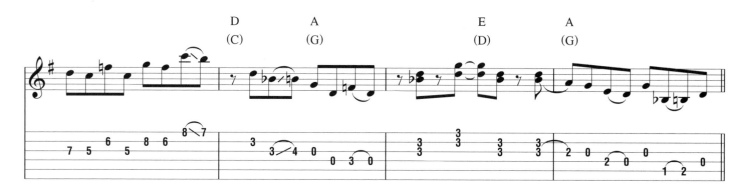

Fiddle Solo

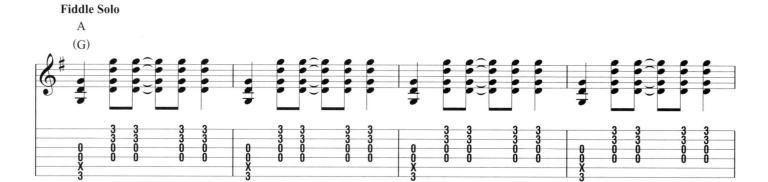

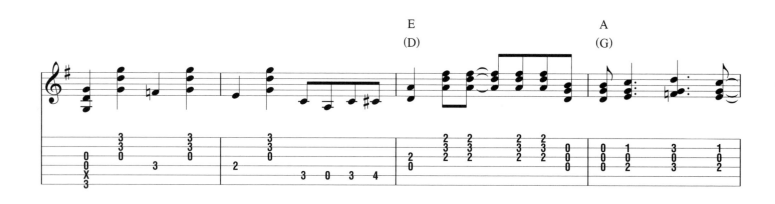

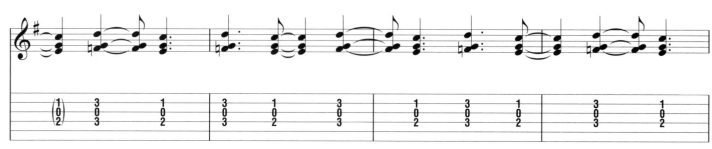

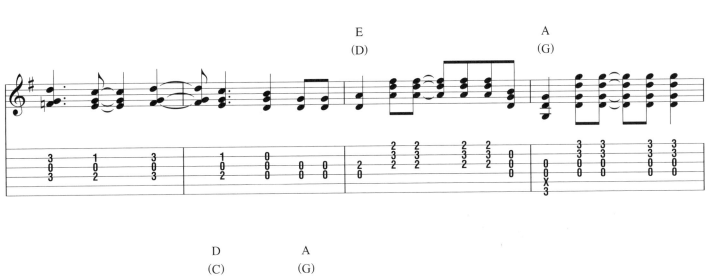

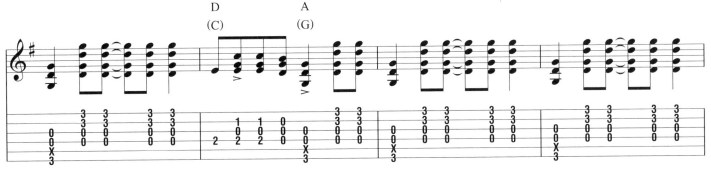

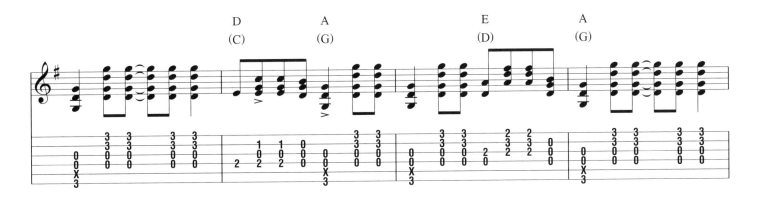

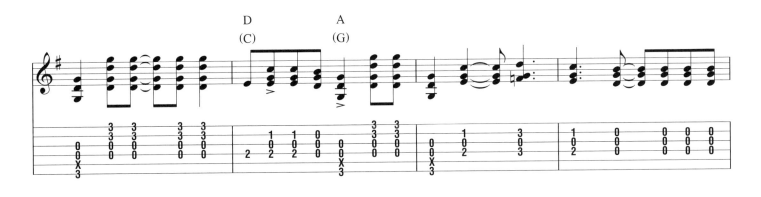

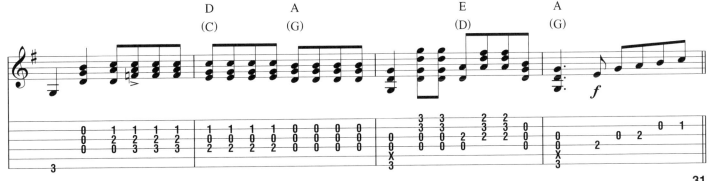

Theme

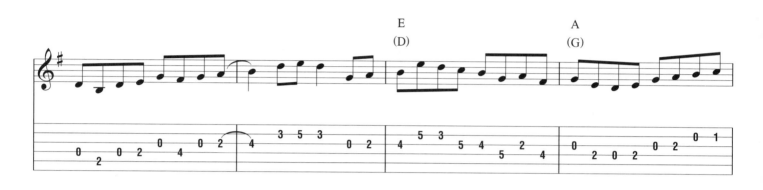

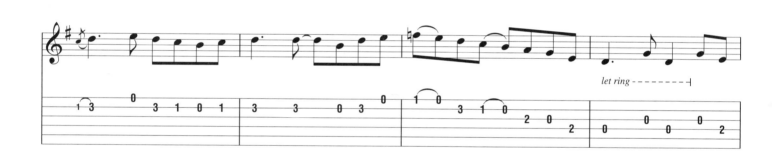

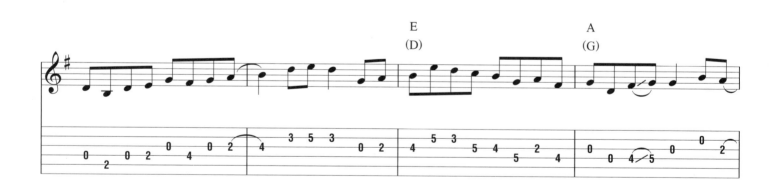

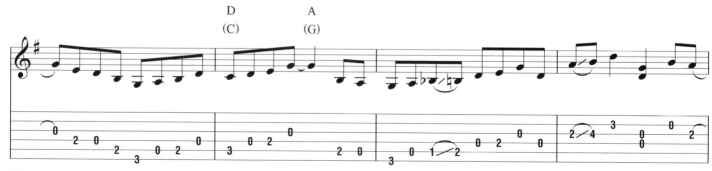

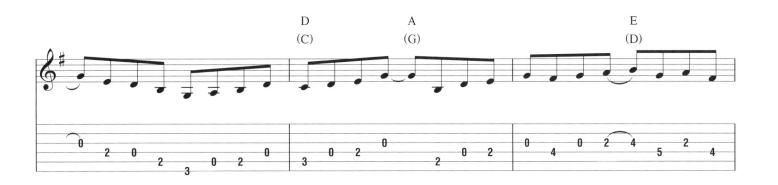
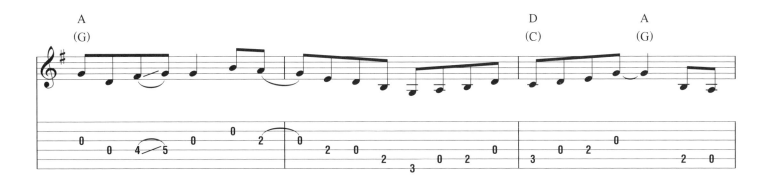

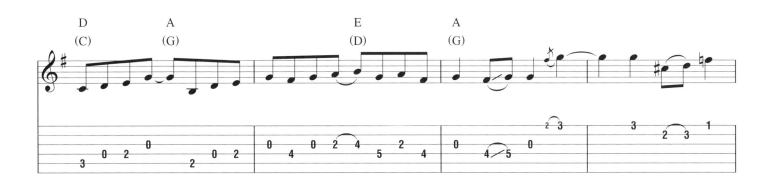
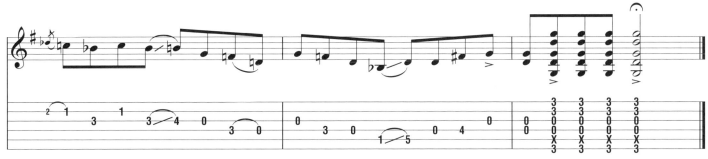

Nine Pound Hammer

Words and Music by Merle Travis

*Downward-stemmed notes w/ P.M. & played w/ thumb throughout.

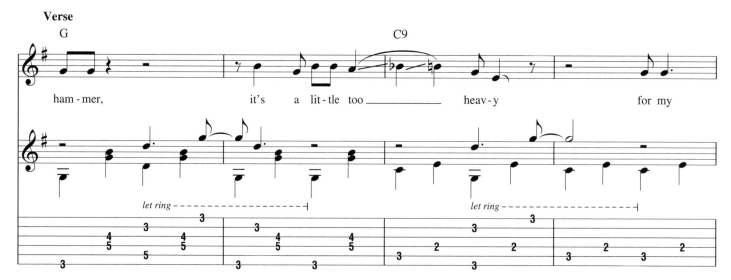

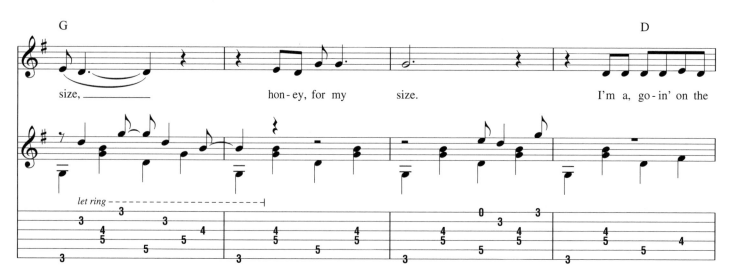

Verse

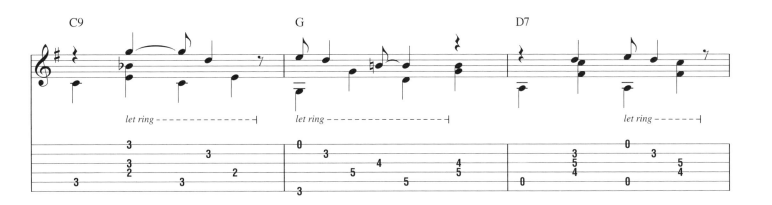

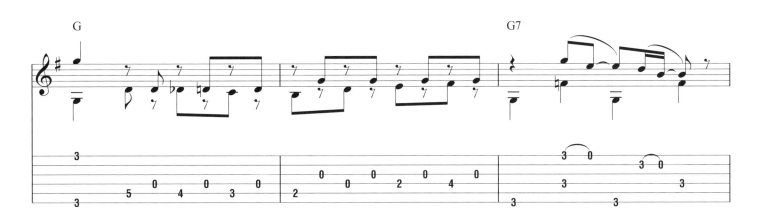

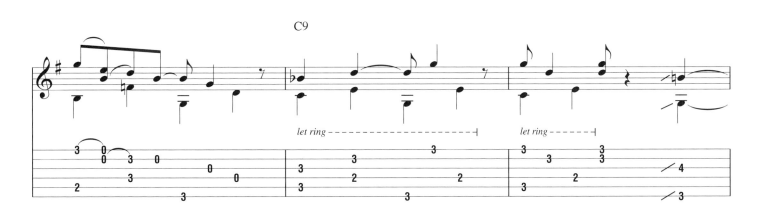

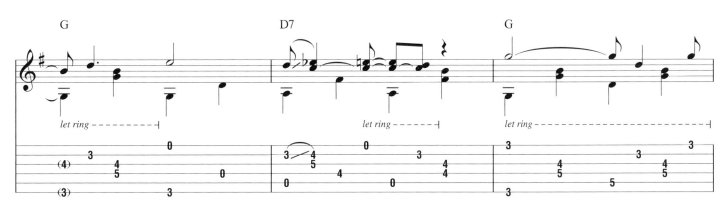

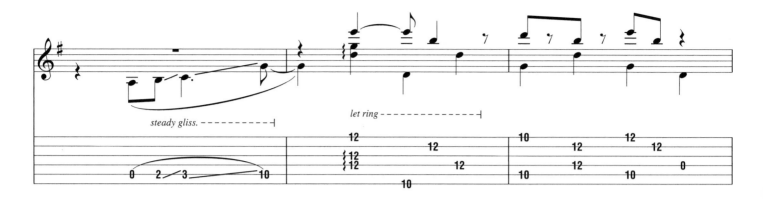

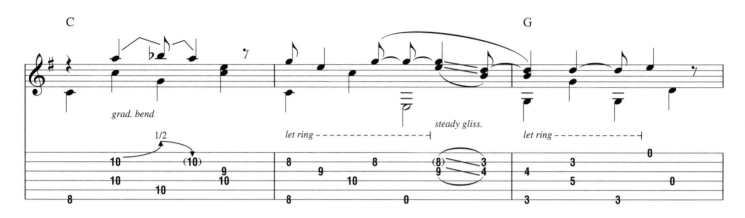

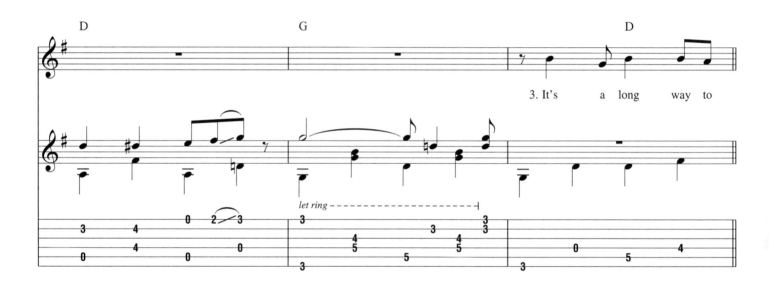

3. It's a long way to

Verse

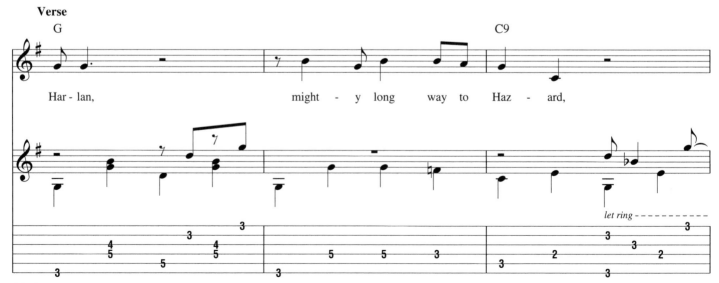

Har - lan, might - y long way to Haz - ard,

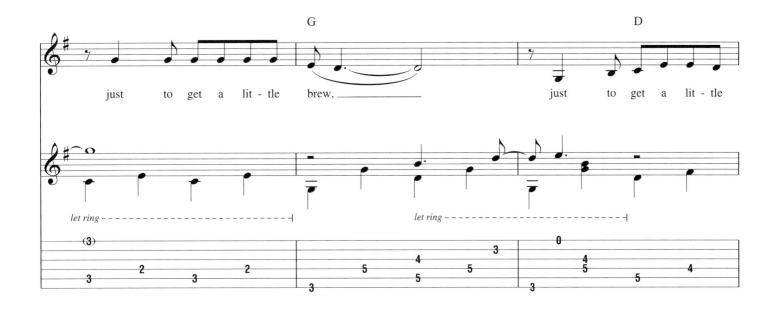

just to get a lit - tle brew, _____ just to get a lit - tle

brew. Well, when I'm long _____ gone, _

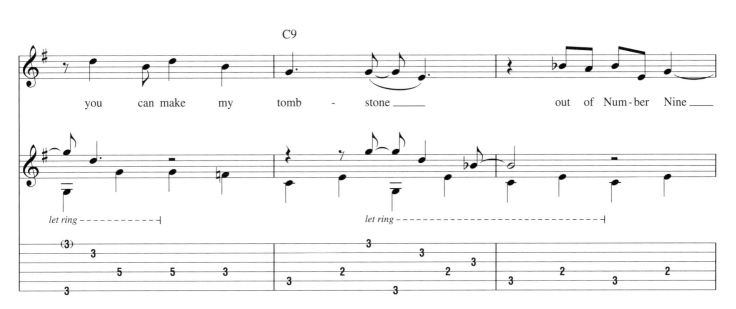

you can make my tomb - stone _____ out of Num - ber Nine _____

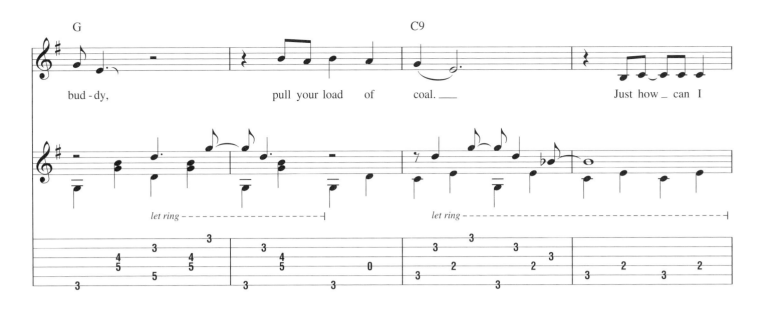

bud - dy,   pull your load of coal. ___   Just how _ can I

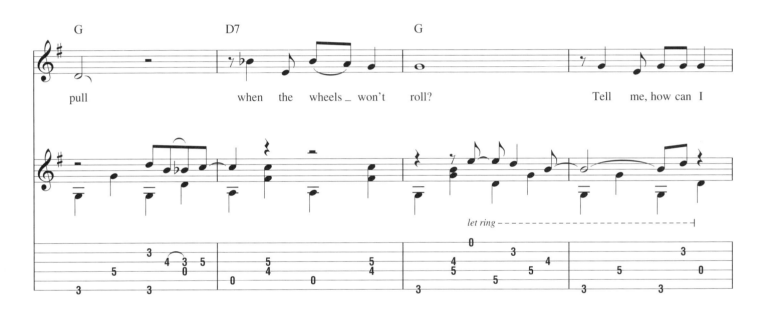

pull   when the wheels _ won't roll?   Tell me, how can I

pull _   when the wheels _ won't roll? _____

Orange Blossom Special

Words and Music by Ervin T. Rouse

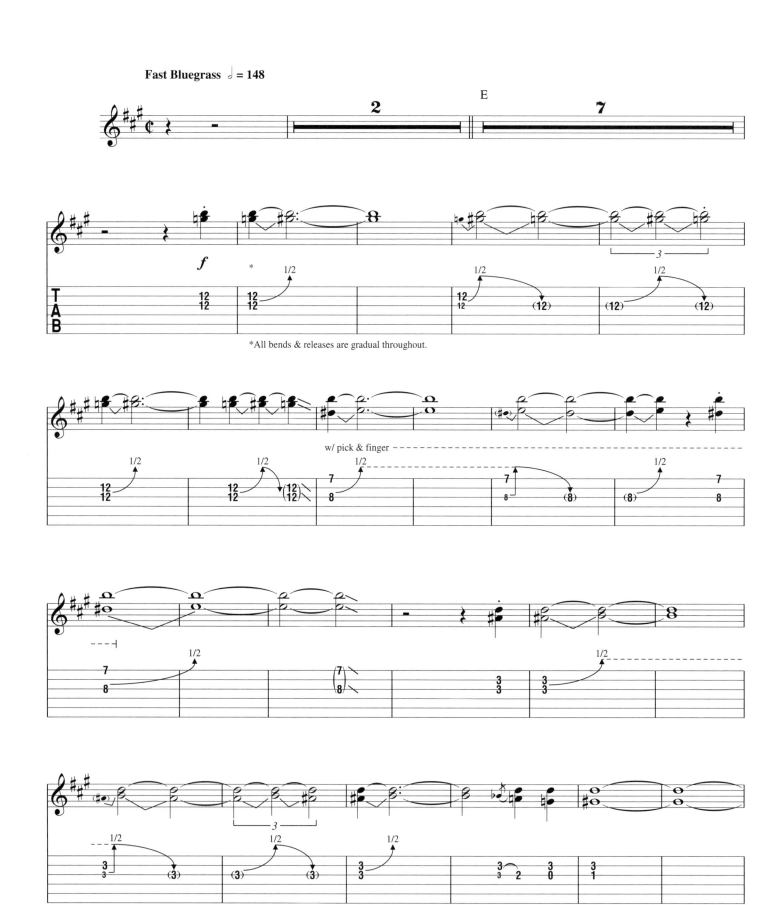

*All bends & releases are gradual throughout.

w/ pick & finger

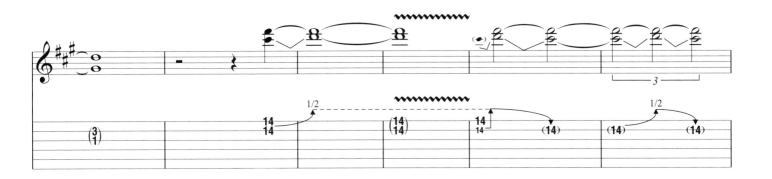
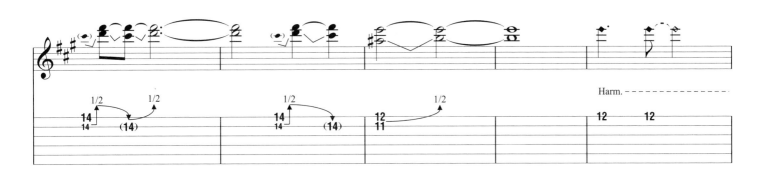
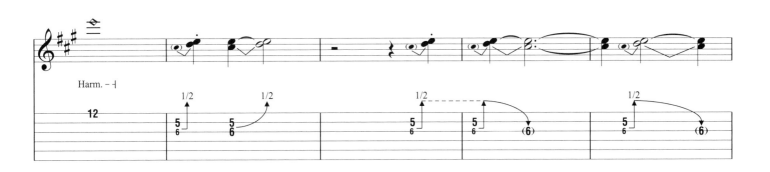

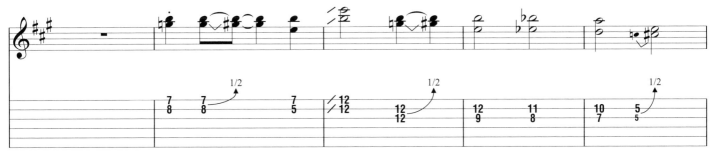

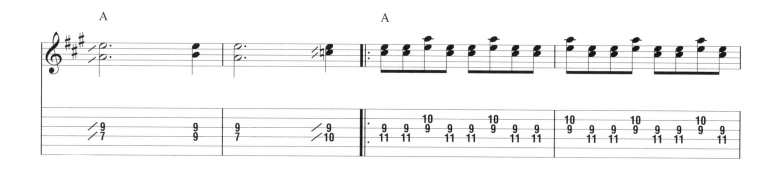

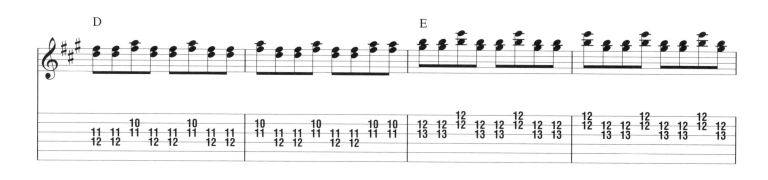

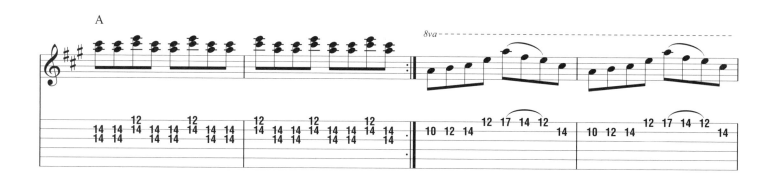

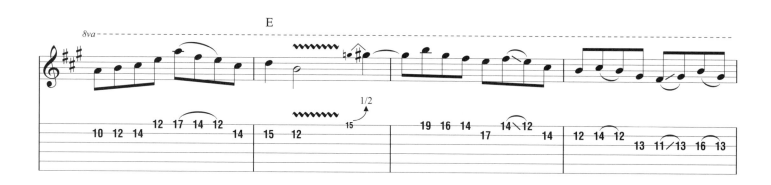

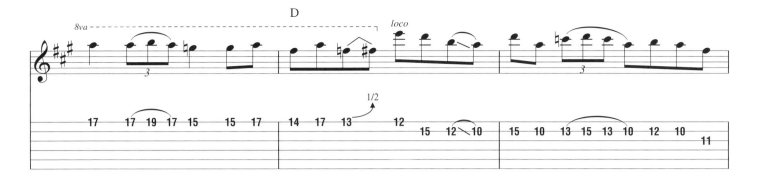

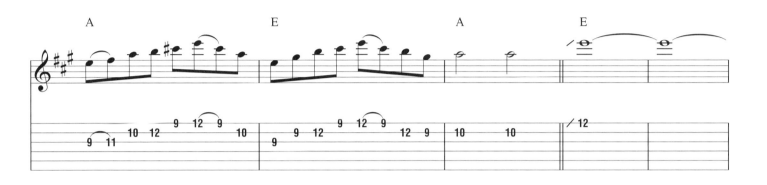

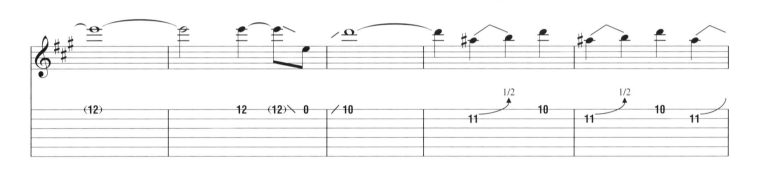

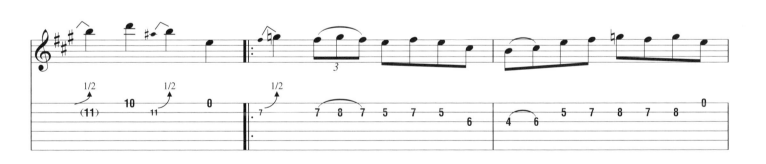

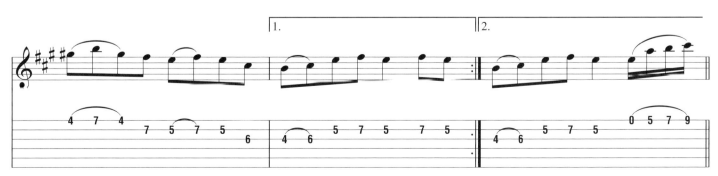

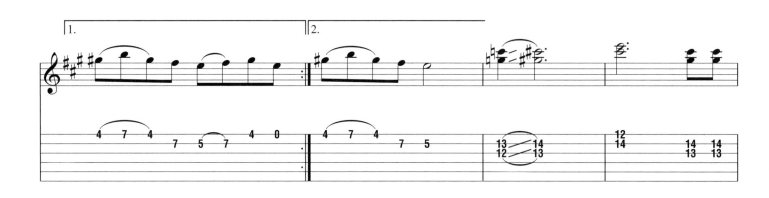

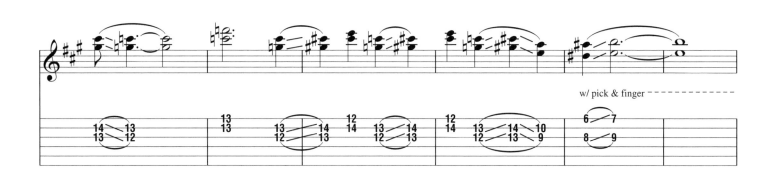

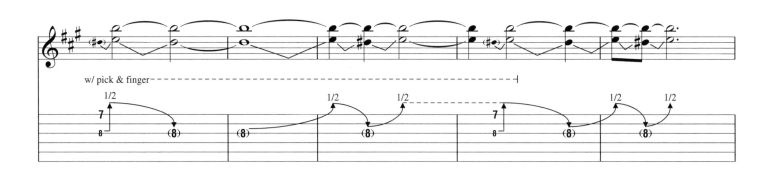

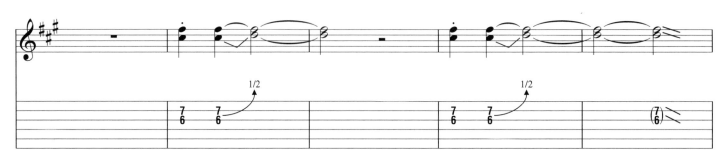

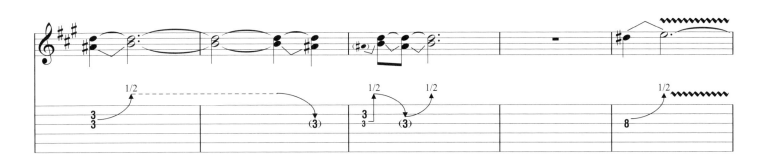

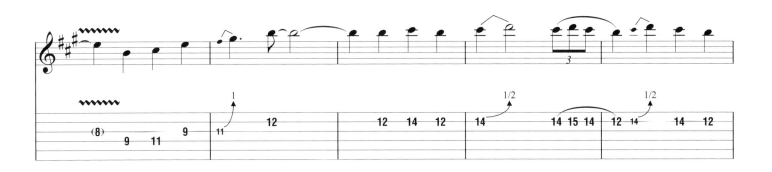

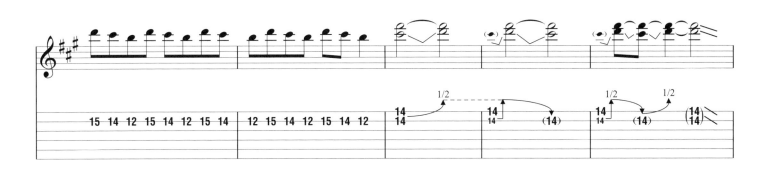

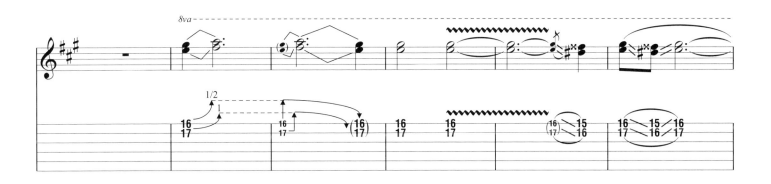

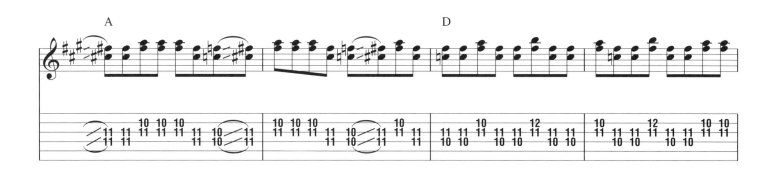

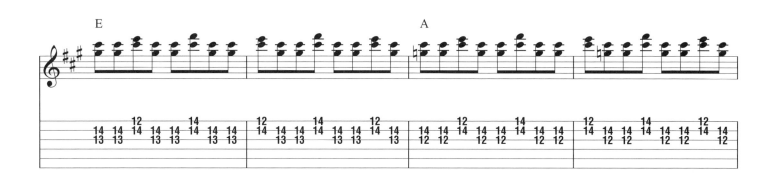

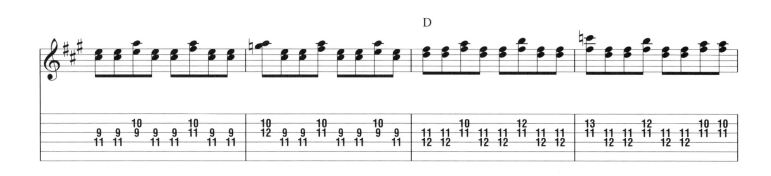

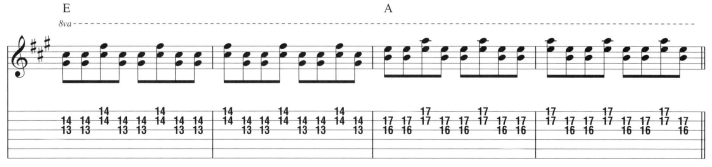

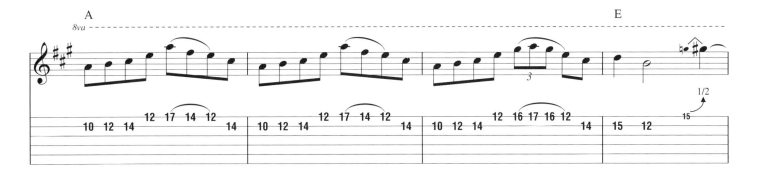
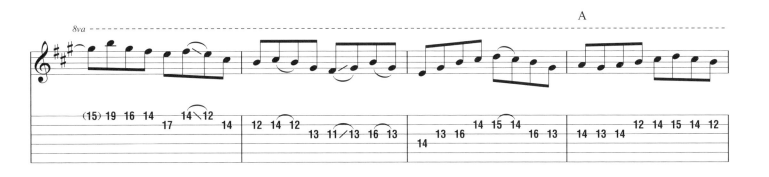
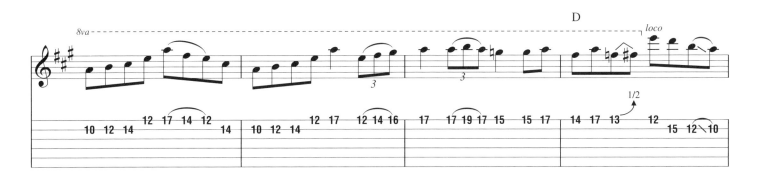
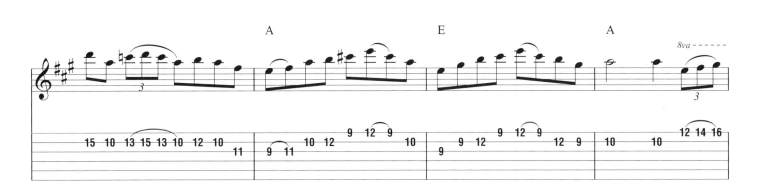
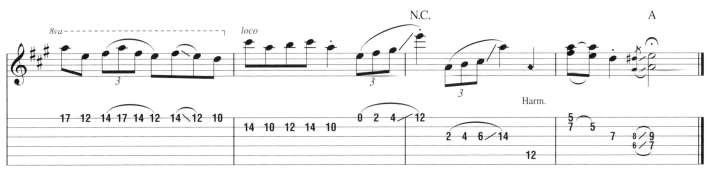

Wildwood Flower

Words and Music by A.P. Carter

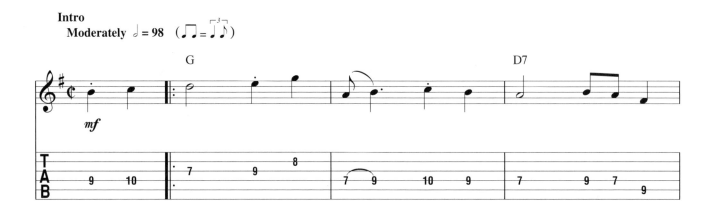

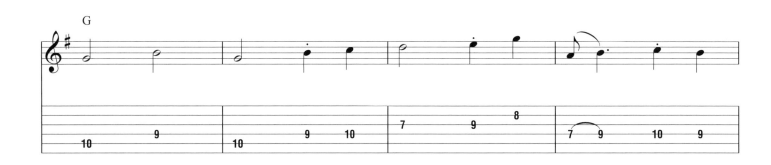

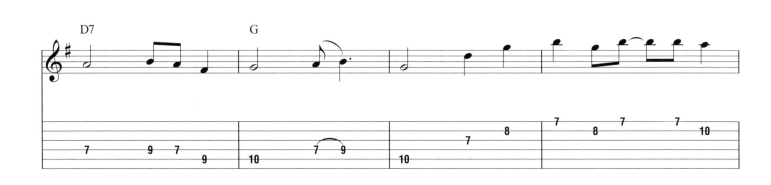

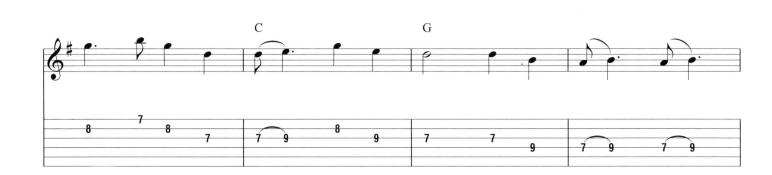

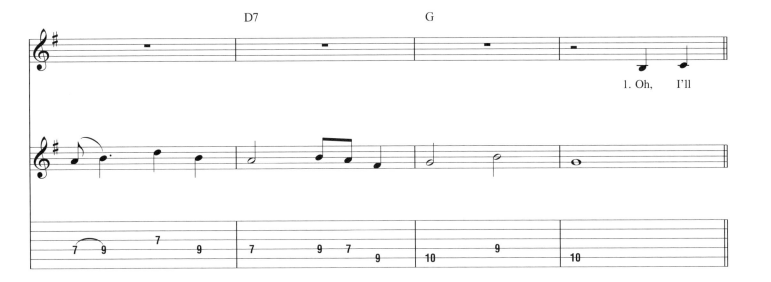

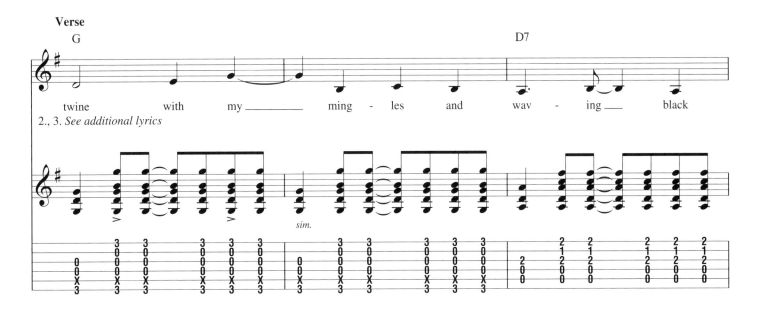

Verse

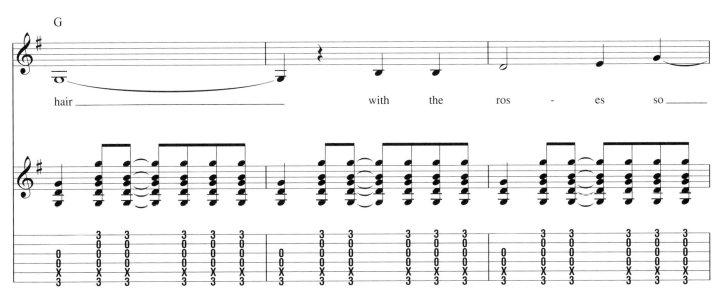

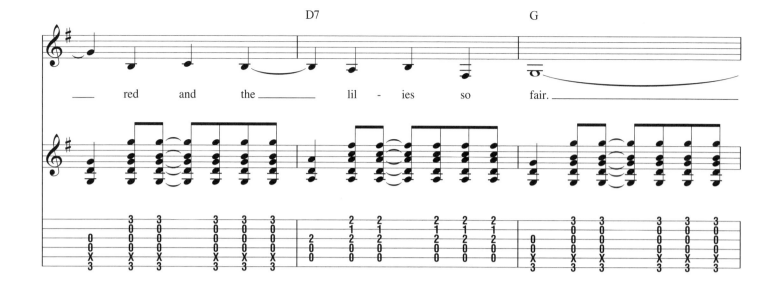

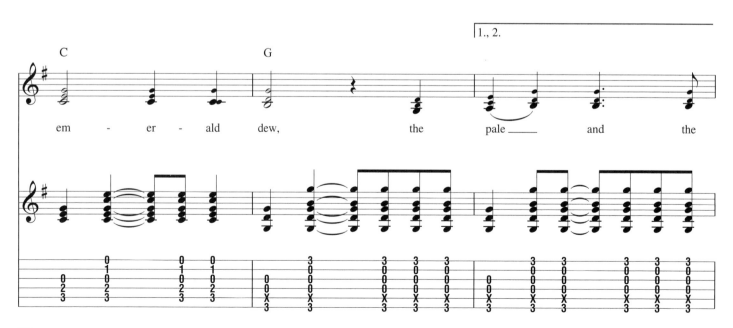

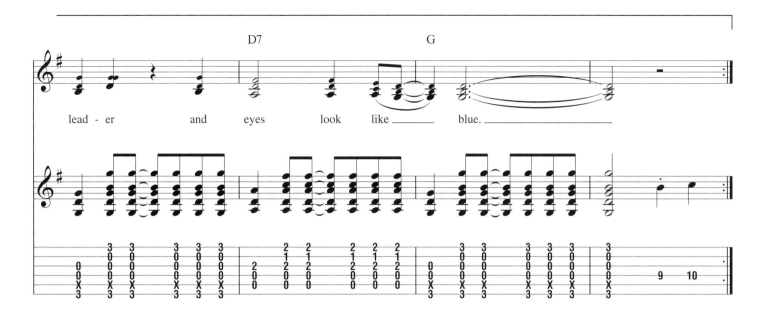

leader and eyes look like _____ blue. _____

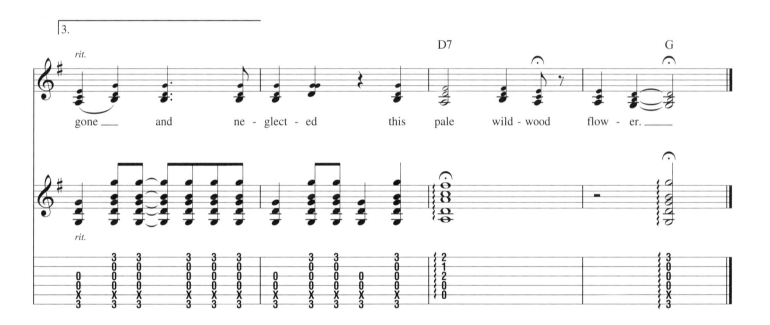

gone ____ and ne - glect - ed this pale wild - wood flow - er. ____

Additional Lyrics

2. Oh, he taught me to love him and promised to love
   And to cherish me over all others above.
   How my heart is now wondering, no misery can tell.
   He's left me no warning, no words of farewell.

3. Oh, he taught me to love him and called me his flower,
   That was blooming to cheer him through life's dreary hour.
   Oh, I long to see him and regret the dark hour.
   He's gone and neglected this pale wildwood flower.

Rocky Top

Words and Music by Boudleaux Bryant and Felice Bryant

Capo IV

Intro
Fast Bluegrass ♩ = 158

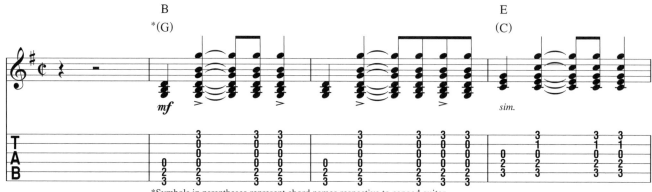

*Symbols in parentheses represent chord names respective to capoed guitar.
Symbols above represent actual sounding chords. Capoed fret is "0" in tab.

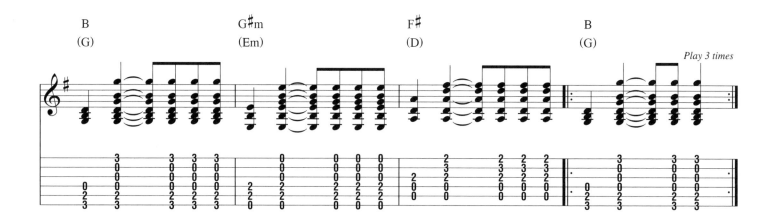

𝄋 Verse

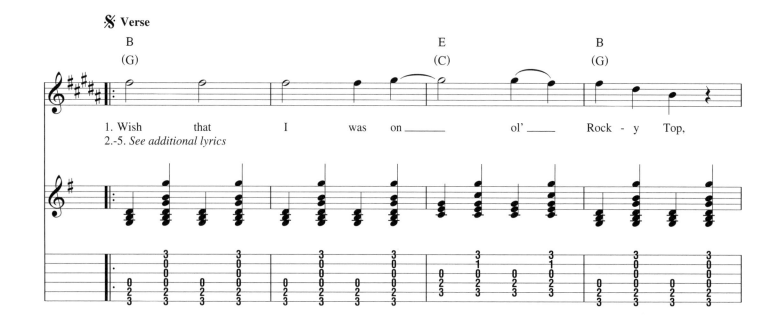

1. Wish that I was on _____ ol' _____ Rock - y Top,
2.-5. *See additional lyrics*

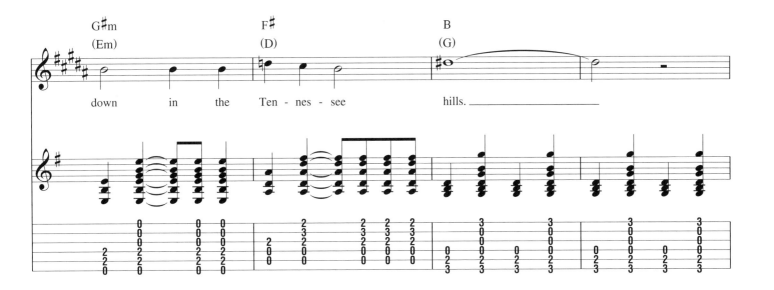

down in the Ten - nes - see hills. _____

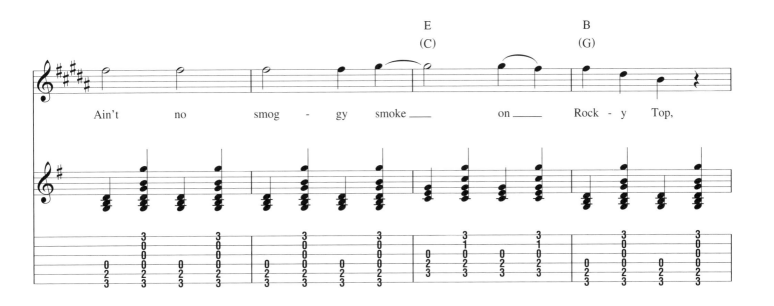

Ain't no smog - gy smoke ___ on ___ Rock - y Top,

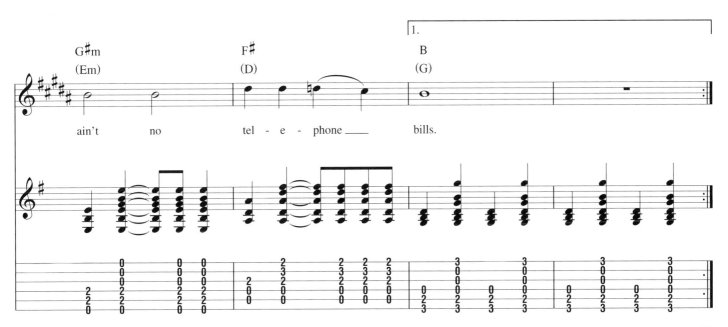

ain't no tel - e - phone ___ bills.

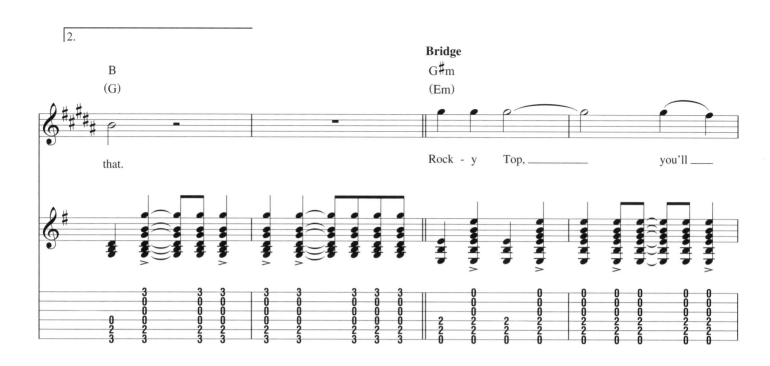

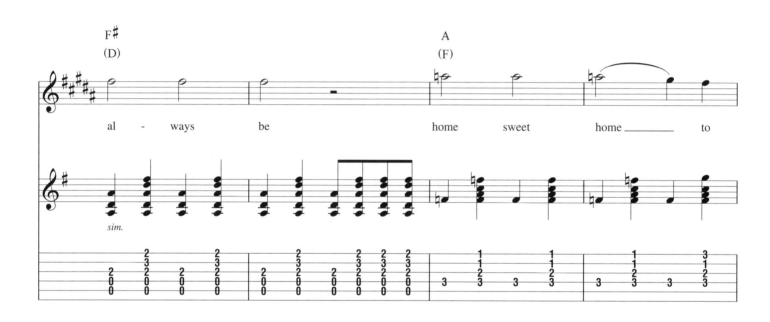

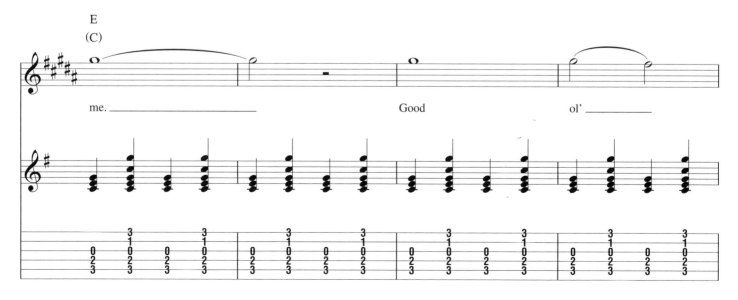

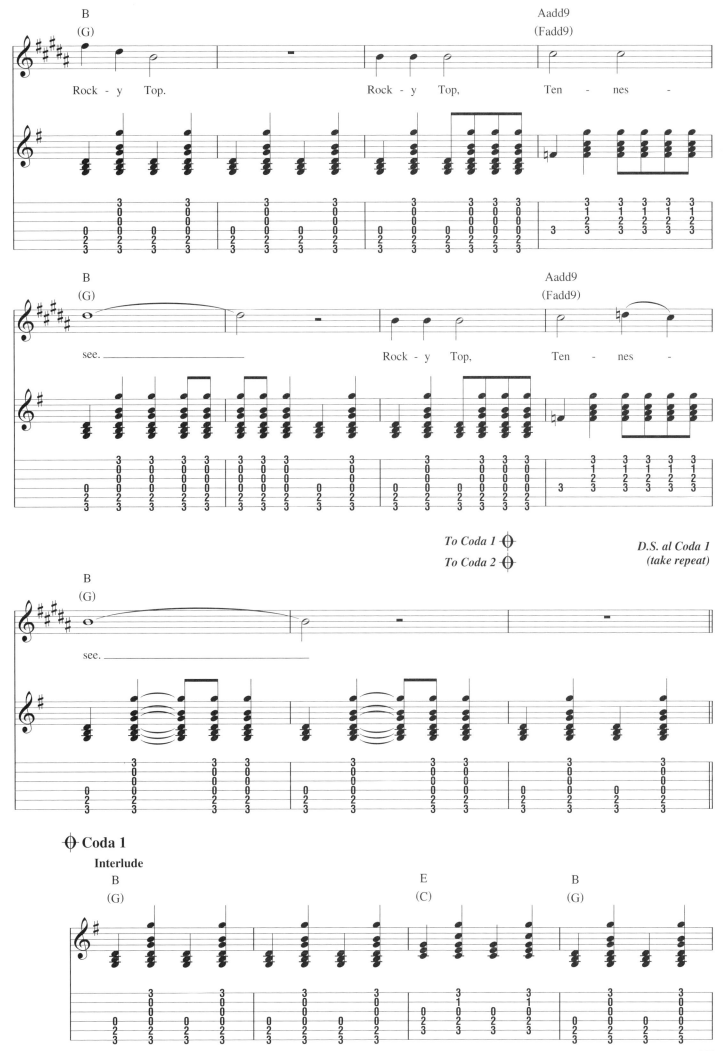

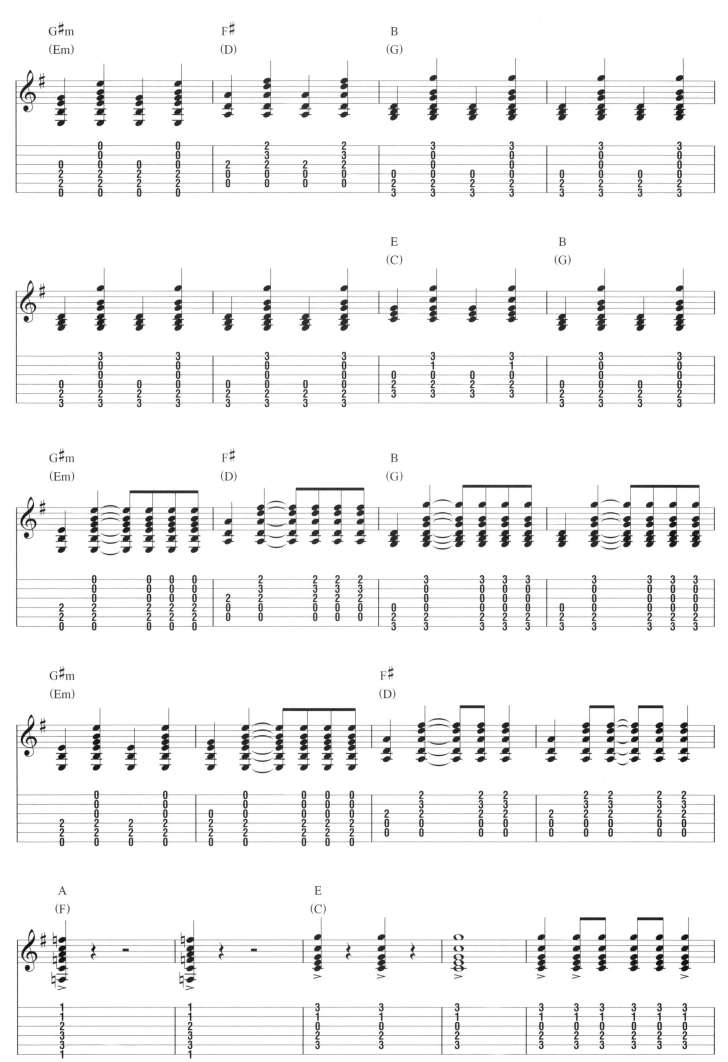

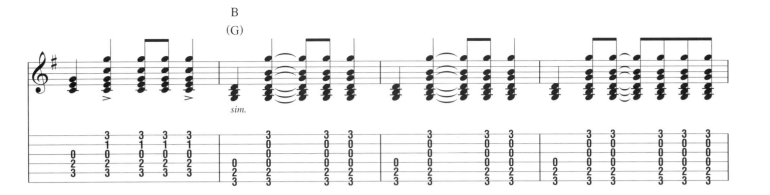

Aadd9
(Fadd9)
B
(G)

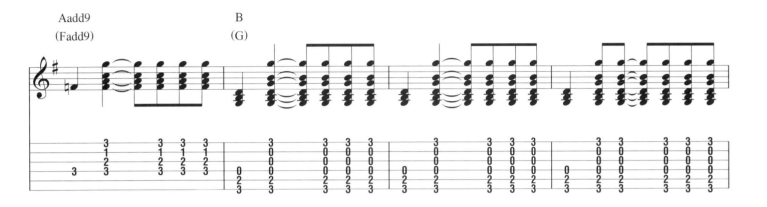

D.S. al Coda 2
(take 2nd ending)

Aadd9
(Fadd9)
B
(G)

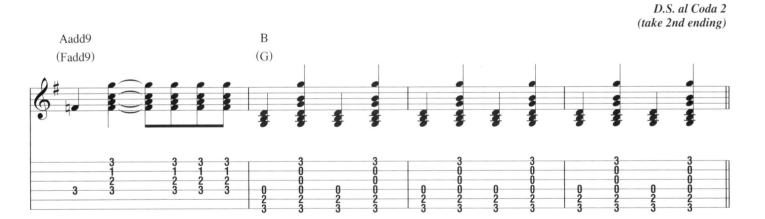

$\oplus$ **Coda 2**

Rock - y Top, Ten - nes - see. _____

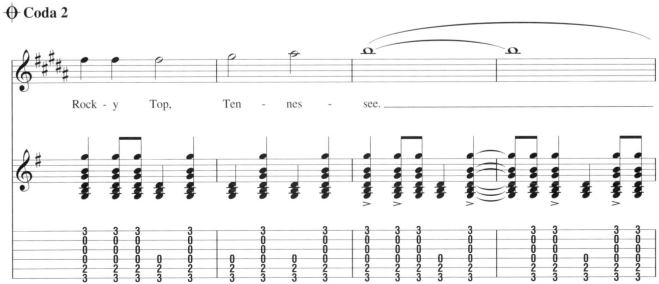

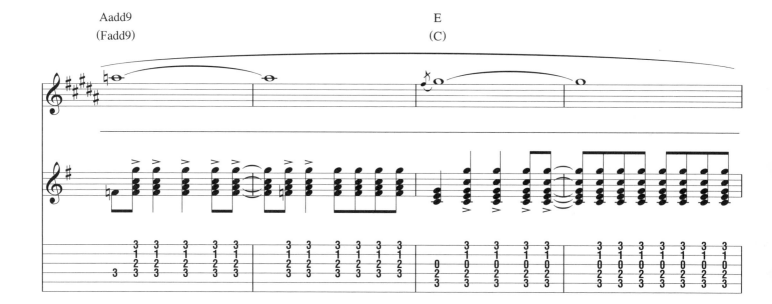

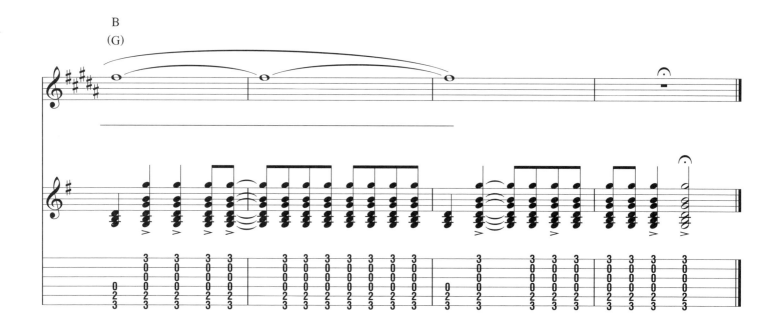

Additional Lyrics

2. Once I had a girl on Rocky Top,
   Half bear, the other half cat.
   Wild as a mink but sweet as soda pop;
   I still dream about that.

3. Once two strangers climbed ol' Rocky Top
   Lookin' for a moonshine still.
   Strangers ain't come down from Rocky Top;
   Reckon they never will.

4. The corn won't grow at all on Rocky Top,
   Dirt's too rocky by far.
   That's why all the folks on Rocky Top
   Get their corn from a jar.

5. I've had years of cramped-up city life,
   Trapped like a duck in a pen.
   All I know is it's a pity life
   Can't be simple again.

GUITAR NOTATION LEGEND

THE MUSICAL STAFF shows pitches and rhythms and is divided by bar lines into measures. Pitches are named after the first seven letters of the alphabet.

TABLATURE graphically represents the guitar fingerboard. Each horizontal line represents a string, and each number represents a fret.

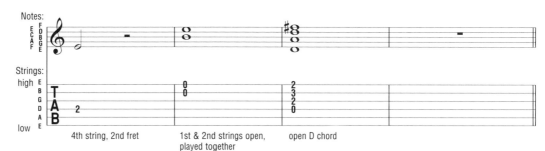

4th string, 2nd fret | 1st & 2nd strings open, played together | open D chord

HALF-STEP BEND: Strike the note and bend up 1/2 step.

WHOLE-STEP BEND: Strike the note and bend up one step.

GRACE NOTE BEND: Strike the note and immediately bend up as indicated.

SLIGHT (MICROTONE) BEND: Strike the note and bend up 1/4 step.

BEND AND RELEASE: Strike the note and bend up as indicated, then release back to the original note. Only the first note is struck.

PRE-BEND: Bend the note as indicated, then strike it.

VIBRATO: The string is vibrated by rapidly bending and releasing the note with the fretting hand.

PALM MUTING: The note is partially muted by the pick hand lightly touching the string(s) just before the bridge.

HAMMER-ON: Strike the first (lower) note with one finger, then sound the higher note (on the same string) with another finger by fretting it without picking.

PULL-OFF: Place both fingers on the notes to be sounded. Strike the first note and without picking, pull the finger off to sound the second (lower) note.

LEGATO SLIDE: Strike the first note and then slide the same fret-hand finger up or down to the second note. The second note is not struck.

SHIFT SLIDE: Same as legato slide, except the second note is struck.

TRILL: Very rapidly alternate between the notes indicated by continuously hammering on and pulling off.

TAPPING: Hammer ("tap") the fret indicated with the pick-hand index or middle finger and pull off to the note fretted by the fret hand.

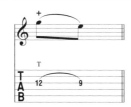

NATURAL HARMONIC: Strike the note while the fret-hand lightly touches the string directly over the fret indicated.

PINCH HARMONIC: The note is fretted normally and a harmonic is produced by adding the edge of the thumb or the tip of the index finger of the pick hand to the normal pick attack.

TREMOLO PICKING: The note is picked as rapidly and continuously as possible.

VIBRATO BAR DIVE AND RETURN: The pitch of the note or chord is dropped a specified number of steps (in rhythm), then returned to the original pitch.

VIBRATO BAR SCOOP: Depress the bar just before striking the note, then quickly release the bar.

VIBRATO BAR DIP: Strike the note and then immediately drop a specified number of steps, then release back to the original pitch.

Additional Musical Definitions

(accent) • Accentuate note (play it louder).

(staccato) • Play the note short.

D.S. al Coda • Go back to the sign (%), then play until the measure marked "***To Coda***," then skip to the section labelled "**Coda**."

D.C. al Fine • Go back to the beginning of the song and play until the measure marked "***Fine***" (end).

Fill • Label used to identify a brief melodic figure which is to be inserted into the arrangement.

N.C. • Harmony is implied.

• Repeat measures between signs.

• When a repeated section has different endings, play the first ending only the first time and the second ending only the second time.

Hal • Leonard GUITAR PLAY-ALONG

INCLUDES TAB

This series will help you play your favorite songs quickly and easily. Just follow the tab and listen to the CD to hear how the guitar should sound, and then play along using the separate backing tracks. Mac or PC users can also slow down the tempo without changing pitch by using the CD in their computer. The melody and lyrics are included in the book so that you can sing or simply follow along.

57. SYSTEM OF A DOWN 00699751...............................$14.95	**71. CHRISTIAN ROCK** 00699824...............................$14.95	**87. ACOUSTIC WOMEN** 00700763 ....$14.99	**111. JOHN MELLENCAMP** 00701056 ....$14.99
58. BLINK-182 00699772...............................$14.95	**72. ACOUSTIC '90s** 00699827...............................$14.95	**88. GRUNGE** 00700467...............................$16.99	**113. JIM CROCE** 00701058...............................$14.99
59. GODSMACK 00699773...............................$14.95	**73. BLUESY ROCK** 00699829 ....$16.99	**91. BLUES INSTRUMENTALS** 00700505...............................$14.99	**114. BON JOVI** 00701060 ....$14.99
60. 3 DOORS DOWN 00699774...............................$14.95	**74. PAUL BALOCHE** 00699831...............................$14.95	**92. EARLY ROCK INSTRUMENTALS** 00700506...............................$12.99	**115. JOHNNY CASH** 00701070 ....$14.99
61. SLIPKNOT 00699775...............................$14.95	**75. TOM PETTY** 00699882...............................$16.99	**93. ROCK INSTRUMENTALS** 00700507...............................$14.99	**116. THE VENTURES** 00701124 ....$14.99
62. CHRISTMAS CAROLS 00699798...............................$12.95	**76. COUNTRY HITS** 00699884...............................$14.95	**96. THIRD DAY** 00700560...............................$14.95	**119. AC/DC CLASSICS** 00701356 ....$14.99
63. CREEDENCE CLEARWATER REVIVAL 00699802...............................$16.99	**78. NIRVANA** 00700132...............................$14.95	**97. ROCK BAND** 00700703...............................$14.99	
64. OZZY OSBOURNE 00699803...............................$16.99	**88. ACOUSTIC ANTHOLOGY** 00700175...............................$19.95	**98. ROCK BAND** 00700704...............................$14.95	*Prices, contents, and availability subject to change without notice.*
65. THE DOORS 00699806...............................$16.99	**81. ROCK ANTHOLOGY** 00700176...............................$22.99	**99. ZZ TOP** 00700762...............................$14.99	FOR MORE INFORMATION, SEE YOUR LOCAL MUSIC DEALER, OR WRITE TO:
66. THE ROLLING STONES 00699807...............................$16.95	**82. EASY ROCK SONGS** 00700177...............................$12.99	**100. B.B. KING** 00700466...............................$14.99	
67. BLACK SABBATH 00699808...............................$16.99	**83. THREE CHORD SONGS** 00700178...............................$14.99	**103. SWITCHFOOT** 00700773...............................$16.99	
68. PINK FLOYD – DARK SIDE OF THE MOON 00699809...............................$16.99	**84. STEELY DAN** 00700200...............................$16.99	**106. WEEZER** 00700958...............................$14.99	**HAL•LEONARD®** CORPORATION 7777 W. BLUEMOUND RD. P.O. BOX 13819 MILWAUKEE, WISCONSIN 53213
69. ACOUSTIC FAVORITES 00699810...............................$14.95	**85. THE POLICE** 00700269 ....$16.99	**108. THE WHO** 00701053 ....$14.99	**For complete songlists, visit Hal Leonard online at www.halleonard.com**
70. OZZY OSBOURNE 00699805 ....$16.99	**86. BOSTON** 00700465 ....$16.99	**109. STEVE MILLER** 00701054 ....$14.99	0710

Presenting the Best in
BLUEGRASS

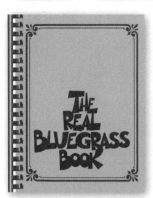

THE REAL BLUEGRASS BOOK

This new collection gathers over 150 bluegrass favorites presented in the world-famous Real Book format. Songs include: Ballad of Jed Clampett • Bill Cheatham • Down to the River to Pray • Foggy Mountain Top • I'm Goin' Back to Old Kentucky • John Henry • Old Train • Pretty Polly • Rocky Top • Sally Goodin • Wildwood Flower • and more.

00310910 C Instruments....................... $29.99

BLUEGRASS

Guitar Play-Along

The Guitar Play-Along Series will help you play your favorite songs quickly and easily! Just follow the tab, listen to the CD to hear how the guitar should sound, and then play along using the separate backing tracks. 8 songs: Duelin' Banjos • Foggy Mountain Breakdown • Gold Rush • I Am a Man of Constant Sorrow • Nine Pound Hammer • Orange Blossom Special • Rocky Top • Wildwood Flower.

00699910 Book/CD Pack...................... $12.99

BLUEGRASS GUITAR CLASSICS

22 CARTER-STYLE SOLOS

Includes standard notation and tab for 22 Carter-style solos from bluegrass classics such as: Back Up and Push • The Big Rock Candy Mountain • Cotton Eyed Joe • Down Yonder • Jesse James • John Henry • Little Sadie • Man of Constant Sorrow • Midnight Special • Mule Skinner Blues • Red Wing • Uncle Joe • The Wabash Cannon Ball • Wildwood Flower • and more.

00699529 .... $7.95

BLUEGRASS GUITAR

Arranged and Performed by Wayne Henderson
Transcribed by David Ziegele

This book/CD pack contains 10 classic bluegrass tunes arranged for solo flatpicking and fingerstyle guitar, in standard notation and tab. The CD features renowned picker Wayne Henderson performing each tune note for note. Includes: Black Mountain Rag • Fisher's Hornpipe • Leather Britches • Lime Rock • Sally Anne • Take Me Out to the Ball Game • Temperence Reel • Twinkle Little Star • and more.

00700184 Book/CD Pack...................... $16.99

BLUEGRASS STANDARDS

by David Hamburger

16 bluegrass classics expertly arranged: Ballad of Jed Clampett • Blue Yodel No. 4 (California Blues) • Can't You Hear Me Calling • I'll Go Stepping Too • I'm Goin' Back to Old Kentucky • Let Me Love You One More Time • My Rose of Old Kentucky • We'll Meet Again Sweetheart • and more.

00699760....................................$7.99

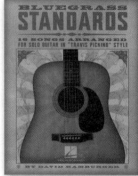

FRETBOARD ROADMAPS – BLUEGRASS AND FOLK GUITAR

by Fred Sokolow

This book/CD pack will have you playing lead and rhythm anywhere on the fretboard, in any key. You'll learn chord-based licks, moveable major and blues scales, major pentatonic "sliding scales," first-position major scales, and moveable-position major scales. The book includes easy-to-follow diagrams and instructions for beginning, intermediate and advanced players. The CD includes 41 demonstration tracks.

00695355 Book/CD Pack...................... $12.95

THE BIG BOOK OF BLUEGRASS SONGS

The best collection ever of 70+ bluegrass standards! Includes: Alabama Jubilee • Arkansas Traveler • Blue Yodel No. 8 • Cripple Creek • Dark Holler • I Am a Man of Constant Sorrow • I Saw the Light • Orange Blossom Special • Rocky Top • Wayfaring Stranger • Will the Circle Be Unbroken • You Don't Know My Mind • and more.

00311484... $19.95

O BROTHER, WHERE ART THOU?

This songbook features nine selections from the critically-acclaimed Coen brothers film, arranged in melody/lyric/chord format with guitar tab. Songs include: Big Rock Candy Mountain (Harry McClintock) • You Are My Sunshine (Norman Blake) • Hard Time Killing Floor Blues (Chris Thomas King) • I Am a Man of Constant Sorrow (The Soggy Bottom Boys/ Norman Blake) • Keep on the Sunny Side (The Whites) • I'll Fly Away (Alison Krauss and Gillian Welch) • and more.

00313182... $17.95

FOR MORE INFORMATION, SEE YOUR LOCAL MUSIC DEALER,
OR WRITE TO:

HAL•LEONARD®
CORPORATION

7777 W. BLUEMOUND RD. P.O. BOX 13819 MILWAUKEE, WI 53213

Prices, contents, and availability subject to change.